Bill Ho███████OL

Teaching Our Children to Read

The Role of Skills in a Comprehensive Reading Program

CORWIN PRESS, INC.
A Sage Publications Company
Thousand Oaks, California

A preliminary report titled "How Should We Teach Our Children to Read?" was released in Summer 1995 by Far West Laboratory for Educational Research and Development (now WestEd), San Francisco, CA.

For information address:

Corwin Press, Inc.
A Sage Publications Company
2455 Teller Road
Thousand Oaks, California 91320
E-mail: order@corwin.sagepub.com

SAGE Publications Ltd.
6 Bonhill Street
London EC2A 4PU
United Kingdom

SAGE Publications India Pvt. Ltd.
M-32 Market
Greater Kailash I
New Delhi 110 048 India

Printed in the United States of America

Library of Congress Cataloging-in-Publication Data

Honig, Bill.
   Teaching our children to read: The role of skills in a comprehensive reading program / author, Bill Honig.
     p. cm.
   Includes bibliographical references and index.
   ISBN 0-8039-6404-8 (acid-free paper). — ISBN 0-8039-6405-6 (pbk.: acid-free paper)
   1. Reading.   2. Reading (Elementary)   I. Title.
LB1050.H64   1996
372.4'14—dc20   95-41752

This book is printed on acid-free paper.

96 97 98 99   10 9 8 7 6 5 4 3 2 1

Corwin Press Production Editor: Diana E. Axelsen
Corwin Press Typesetter: Christina M. Hill

Contents

Preface and Acknowledgments — vii

About the Author — viii

1. The Case for a Balanced Approach — 1

The Great Debate / 2
Contributions of the Whole-Language Movement / 3
Whole-Language Myths / 4
Successful Early Reading Programs in Practice / 8
Essential Components of an Effective Literacy
    Strategy / 9
Comprehensive and Balanced: Not the Same
    as Eclectic / 11
Summary / 13

2. What Skilled Readers Do — 16

The Importance of Seeing Letter Combinations
    in Words / 16
The Mental Mechanisms of Reading Proficiency / 18
Skills Needed to Become a Proficient Reader / 20

3. Beginning-to-Read Instruction for Preschool
   and Kindergarten — 25

Listening to Stories, Discussing Them, and Oral Expression—
    at School and at Home / 26
Naming and Recognizing Letters / 27
The Importance of Phonemic Awareness / 29
Print Awareness / 34
Mastering a Few Sight Words / 35
Syntactic Awareness / 35
Summary / 35

4. **Beginning-to-Read Instruction for Early First Grade**   39

The Learning-to-Read Sequence / 41
Recognizing Single Words / 41
Learning to Decode / 42
Reading and Comprehension / 44
Practice Makes Perfect: The Sequence of Becoming
     an Automatic Reader / 45
Early First-Grade Reading Components
     and Instruction / 50
Individual Diagnosis and Benchmarks:
     Keys to Effective Instruction / 65
Practicing Skills While Reading for Meaning
     With a Teacher, Adult, or Student Partner / 66
Specifically Designed Books and Materials / 67
Correctness Versus Coverage / 69
The Importance of Timely, Early Intervention / 70
Individual and Group Tutoring / 71
Successful Reading Programs in the Classroom / 72
Grouping Strategies / 77
Determining Structure / 78

5. **Reading Instruction for Middle First Grade
to Upper Elementary Grades**   83

A Book- and Story-Driven Strategy to Teach Skills / 83
First Principle: Matching Books to Students' Levels / 84
Second Principle: Frequent Evaluation of
     Students' Reading / 85
Continued Letter/Sound, Spelling, and
     Decoding Support / 87
Syllables and Word Roots / 88
Skills Development / 89
Summary / 90

6. **Spelling, Beginning Writing, and Vocabulary**   91

Spelling / 91
Teaching Spelling / 93
Beginning Writing / 98
Vocabulary / 99

7. Comprehension and Assessment   101

    The Read-a-Lot Strategy / 102
    Strategic Reading / 104
    Discussion of Books / 105
    Assessment / 109

8. Writing and Speaking   112

    Written and Oral Applications / 112
    Writing / 113
    Speaking and Listening Skills / 115

9. Frequently Asked Questions   116

10. Conclusions and Lessons Learned   123

Appendix A: The Role of Skills in a Comprehensive
              Elementary Reading Program—
              24 Major Points   125

Appendix B: Reading Skills Curriculum Timeline—
              Preschool Through Fifth Grade   132

References   139

Index   147

This book is dedicated to those teachers, researchers, educators, and leaders who have kept their common sense and are beseeching the educational community to reach an effective, working consensus on how best to teach our children to read. I hope the information provided here—which summarizes and highlights a tremendous amount of research and thinking by the leading experts in the literacy field—will help them achieve this laudable goal

Preface and Acknowledgments

This book represents an attempt to reconcile two concepts in teaching children to read. Both a literature-driven and language-rich language arts program that fosters deep engagement with a text and a comprehensive, organized skill development program that develops fluency and automaticity with print are essential if our students are to be world-class readers. The issues of how to organize classrooms and schools for language-rich activities such as reading to and with children, writing through language experience, teaching listening skills, helping students learn to write, encouraging a love of reading, and providing high-quality books and magazines have been thoroughly explicated in numerous books, articles and texts. What has been missing is a comprehensive compilation of research and best practice on the specifics of skill development and how skills should be organized, taught, and integrated into the language arts program.

That is what I have attempted to do in this book. I hope the information and recommendations contained in this book help those in our profession understand the importance of skill development strands in teaching children to read and provide some guidance on the instructional and curricular issues that must be addressed if we are to successfully integrate whole language principles with the necessary foundation skills and successfully teach all our children to read.

I wish to thank Marilyn Adams, Anne Cunningham, Linda Diamond, Ada Hand, Kate Jamentz, Marion Joseph, Adria Klein, Sheila Mandel, Ruth Nathan, Jerry Treadway, and Dennis Parker for their time in editing this book and their invaluable suggestions. I also wish to thank those many researchers and practitioners who so generously shared their time with me and so willingly shared their ideas and findings. Finally, I wish to thank Far West Laboratory for Educational Research and Development for its editing and technical support.

—Bill Honig
San Francisco State University

About the Author

Bill Honig is a Visiting Distinguished Professor in the School of Education at San Francisco State University and directs the Center for Systemic School Reform at that institution. He was State Superintendent of Public Instruction for the State of California from 1983 to 1993, and under his administration, the State Department of Education issued nationally renowned frameworks in each of the disciplines. Recently, he has been active in the New Standards Project, a collaborative project of states with more than 50% of the nation's children, which is establishing performance standards for English/ Language Arts, Mathematics, Science, and Applied Learning. He is also assisting a large National Science Foundation project in California, the California Alliance for Math and Science, which is working to improve math in more than 400 middle schools and science in nearly 1,000 elementary schools.

Honig also has been active with Far West Laboratory for Educational Research and Development in its efforts to work with schools and districts to improve education, and he has been a member of the group that successfully procured and is administering a joint Walter Annenberg and William Hewlett 5-year grant of $50 million for school improvement in the Bay Area. Most recently, he has been a cofounder of the Coalition on Reading (CORE), 2110 Scott St., San Francisco, CA, (415) 921-8636, which is assisting districts and schools in improving early literacy programs. Honig is the author of *Last Chance for Our Children: How You Can Help Save Our Schools* (1985) and coauthor of the *Handbook for Planning an Effective Reading Program* (1979). He has written numerous articles and been the recipient of several prestigious awards. Honig has been an elementary teacher in central city San Francisco public schools, a school superintendent in Marin County, and a California State Board of Education member. He is married to Nancy Catlin Honig and has four children.

1

The Case for a
Balanced Approach

The first and foremost job of elementary school is to teach children to read. The reading program in every school should enable almost every student to be able to read fluently and understand grade-appropriate material by the end of elementary school, to have read a large number of books, magazines and other informational text, to reach high levels of comprehension ability, and to enjoy and learn from reading. These goals can be achieved only if most students are reading beginning material by mid-first grade. Most students who fail to learn to read by this time are destined to fall further and further behind in school and are effectively prevented from capitalizing on the power of education to improve and enrich their lives. Yet in more and more schools, large numbers of students do not become readers early enough to develop the skills and experience to read age-appropriate materials throughout their elementary careers and are, in effect, excluded from instruction.

Access to further education, high-skilled jobs, and a chance to participate in the higher reaches of society depends in large part on school success, which itself is highly correlated with the ability to read.

1

Given what is known today about the techniques of teaching young-sters to read, no reason exists for this potentially dangerous state of affairs.

Educators must examine current reading practices critically, iden-tify the most successful programs and approaches, and enlist teachers, parents, and leaders responsible for educating our children in the common goal of remedying this unnecessary situation.

The Great Debate

Controversy and confusion in the literacy field today center around how best to teach children to read. Specifically, the question is, Should skills be taught directly in an organized and explicit skills development program as part of beginning-to-read instruction, or will students acquire these skills more indirectly by being read to, immer-sion in print, and learning skills in the context of reading for mean-ing—an approach known as whole language?

Leading experts in the literacy field (Adams, 1990, 1991, 1995; Beck & Juel, 1995; Clay, 1991, 1994; Juel, 1994; Pearson, 1993; Pressley & Rankin, 1994; Share & Stanovich, 1995b; Stahl, 1992; Williams, 1991; see also McPike, 1995, for a good summary) have persuasively argued that, in fact, *we should not be having this destruc-tive controversy about skills-based versus whole-language philosophies of reading at all,* that this is not an "either/or" question. They and a growing number of other experts and top practitioners in reading education advocate a *balanced approach*—one that combines the language- and literature-rich activities associated with whole language aimed at enhancing meaning, understanding, and the love of lan-guage with explicit teaching of the skills needed to develop fluency with print, including the automatic recognition of a growing number of words and the ability to decode new words—for all our chil-dren. (The 24 major points made in this book about the role of skills in a comprehensive elementary reading program are summarized in Appendix A.)

In fact, reading experts who have carefully reviewed the research on approaches to teaching reading agree that whole-language tech-niques *are* a key ingredient of any successful reading program. Almost 30 years ago, Jeanne Chall (1983) exhaustively reviewed the research on beginning-reading programs in her classic 1967 study, *Learning to*

Read: The Great Debate (see also Chall, 1992, 1995). She concluded that beginning-reading programs that emphasized decoding or phonics, the direct and systematic focus on the system that maps print to speech, and the opportunity to practice learning that system in the context of reading were much more effective than those that solely utilized meaning-based approaches. However, at the same time, Chall *also* advocated the language-rich activities promoted by the whole-language movement.

The Contributions of the Whole-Language Movement

Teachers' classroom routines should include reading good literature to students and discussing it with them, especially by asking questions that stretch children's minds beyond the literal meaning of the text. Teachers should fill the classroom with a wide variety of high-quality materials and create a literate environment. Students should have a multitude of opportunities to read along with the teacher, work together on reading and writing activities, write daily, and dictate stories about their interests. Teachers should give students choices in their reading, help them to relate what they know to what they are going to read, assist them in keeping reading logs, and offer them the chance to respond personally to what they have read. (For a summary of classroom activities and organizational strategies to incorporate these ideas, see Depree & Iversen, 1994; for a summary of these techniques, see Smith, 1992.)

These child-centered techniques and the belief that the child is "an active-meaning constructor, an aggressive processor of language and information" (Pearson, 1993, p. 502) are extremely productive in accelerating learning for all children. A recent large-scale study of high-poverty classrooms found that instruction aimed at producing meaning—developing students' capacities to "understand, reason, and compare"—produces higher results than more traditional practices. Knapp, Shields, and Turnbull (1995) define searching for meaning as

Instruction that helps students perceive the relationship of 'parts' (discrete skills) to wholes (e.g., the application of skills to communicate, comprehend, or reason); instruction that provides students with the tools to construct meaning in their encounters with academic tasks and in the world in which they live; and instruction that makes explicit connections between one subject area and the next and between what is learned in school and children's lives. In various ways, teaching for meaning derives from the broader concept of 'teaching for understanding,' which has its roots in cognitive research and constructivist assumptions about teaching and learning [citations omitted]. (p. 771)

The whole-language movement has improved classrooms by promoting practices that encourage students to read outstanding literature including both fiction and, more recently, quality nonfiction; write more; and perceive writing as having a purpose and communicating something important (Pressley & Rankin, 1994, p. 59).

Whole-Language Myths

The crucial issue in reading instruction is whether there *also* should be an organized and directly taught explicit skills development component that stresses decoding words and learning the sound/symbol system. Some of the leaders of the whole-language movement have argued against the inclusion of explicit skills development instruction, claiming that explicit instruction is unnecessary and even harmful. These arguments are without merit.

Myth #1: Children Learn to Read "Naturally"

One argument whole-language advocates put forth is that children will learn to read "naturally" (without direct instruction) from being read to and engaging in other literacy activities, and that breaking up or analyzing words detracts from these natural processes (Goodman, 1976, 1986, 1992 [p. 158]; Smith, 1992; see also Share & Stanovich, 1995b). "Natural learning, according to whole language enthusiasts, does not involve explicit decoding instruction, controlled vocabulary, or any form of instruction; specifically, practice of discrete skills is inimical to the development of mature literacy" (Pressley & Rankin, 1994, p. 158). These advocates contend that children will either intuit the letter/letter pattern/sound/word relationships or recognize the meaning of the word by other methods such as guessing its meaning from the context or shape, and that teachers can fill in skills gaps when they arise.

Unfortunately, these claims have proven false for a significant number of children. In a recent comprehensive review, two top educational researchers, David Share and Keith Stanovich (1995b), surveyed the vast scientific and educational literature and concluded that all these assumptions have been conclusively refuted; guessing from context is not an effective way of learning to read, reading is not acquired naturally in the same way as speech,[1] and analyzing and learning to abstract parts of words does not hinder learning to read—it is indispensable (Foorman, in press; Share & Stanovich, 1995b, pp. 3, 30, 32). Foorman (in press) and Share and Stanovich (1995b) cite numerous studies that have shown that (a) the primary and most efficient strategy for unlocking the meaning of a word is to visually process the letters of that word and that weak readers who cannot decode efficiently tend to overrely on context and (b) guessing an unrecognized word from context clues is an ineffective decoding strategy because it is successful only 10% of the time with content words. Note that the relative effectiveness of using context as the primary method to recognize words, decode new words, and become automatic with words is a different question than whether the use of context accelerates word recognition with accomplished readers. It does (see also Biemiller, 1994).[2]

Moreover, the erroneous belief that almost all students can learn to read without an organized, explicit skill strand has taken root in too many schools and districts with disastrous results. Due to the absence of early, organized skill instruction, a growing number of students are not reaching their optimal levels of reading proficiency. An estimated 30% to 40% of students in many high-poverty areas are remaining, in effect, nonreaders, and significantly more than 50% of students in these areas are not becoming fluent readers of grade-appropriate materials. When these students attempt to study for their lessons in later grades, they will stumble over many words that will prevent them from attending to meaning. Consequently, they will be unable to participate in grade-level instruction and will fall further and further behind during their school careers.

Most of these children will have been barred from becoming fluent readers of grade-level text because they did not receive an organized skills strand early enough to become independent readers of beginning materials in first grade, and thus read enough books successfully to stay on track (Liberman, Shankweiler, & Liberman, 1991). In *Listening to Children Read Aloud: Data From NAEP's Integrated Reading Performance Record (IRPR) at Grade 4,* Pinnell, Pikulski et al. (1995), for example, found that large numbers of fourth graders had very low fluency and reading rates, with reading rates dropping compared to previous years (pp. 21-23, 40-42). If students are not independently reading beginning materials by mid-first grade, they have only a slim chance of reading at grade level by third grade and beyond unless they receive an extraordinary tutoring program (Juel, 1994, p. 125).

Respected educator Lisa Delpit (1995) has noted repeatedly that children from lower socioeconomic families, primarily clustered in urban areas, are especially harmed by the absence of a structured phonics and skills program. Similarly, students with some auditory or memory processing problems—found in all schools and estimated to be as many as 20% of all children—are also especially harmed if a skills strand is missing. For these students, learning to read is a powerful equity issue.

The large subpopulation of students with dyslexia, most of whom are unidentified and situated in regular classrooms, has been extensively studied (Adams, 1990; Liberman et al., 1991; Lyons, 1994, 1995; Moats, 1994).[3] According to the research, most of the students who *are* designated as *learning* disabled and become identified as special education students are really *reading* and *spelling* disabled. In addition, many of the students who have difficulty learning to read, but who are never identified as learning disabled, suffer from the same reading and spelling disability.

The core problem for both of these categories of students is primarily a deficiency in their ability to become aware of and consciously manipulate the phonological (sound) building blocks of language and the units of print that represent them, a skill called phonemic awareness. Most teachers and school policymakers do not understand that a large proportion of their students who are struggling to learn to read are actually suffering from this specific phonological processing difficulty which prevents them from learning phonics and decoding skills and does not allow them to intuit the sound-symbol system. Consequently, many schools fail to provide these students with timely instructional intervention, and, as a result, most of these students will fall significantly and irrevocably behind in reading—*a preventable mishap for all but a few.* Another barrier to timely intervention is the prevailing erroneous opinion that many students in the early grades are not developmentally ready for reading instruction and will "grow out" of their problems with the passage of time.[4]

Other studies support the compelling need for an approach that combines skills and whole-language techniques for special education students. These include Michael Pressley and Joan Rankin's *More About Whole Language Methods of Reading Instruction for Students at Risk for Early Reading Failure* (1994), and the California Department of Education (1994) document, *I Can Learn: A Handbook for Parents, Teachers, and Students,* which discusses the best strategies for these children, summarizes the research, and supports a balanced approach to reading.

Even the 60% to 70% of children who come to school already supported by rich literary experiences, and who eventually will learn to read under any instructional system or philosophy, need supportive skills instruction. Without this support, many will end up reading significantly below their potential in later grades for the following reasons advanced by Adams (1990):

- These children need to review the symbol/sound relationships they have already encountered.
- They need to develop that fragmented knowledge into a systematic understanding of the entire letter/sound system so that they learn how to learn new words by themselves, without having to rely on memorizing them. Children encounter two kinds of new words. They must learn how to read and become fluent with words they have not yet seen in print, but which are in their speaking or listening vocabulary. They also must learn how to read and infer the meaning of words not yet in their spoken vocabulary—words they will encounter with increasing frequency in the later grades—or many will start to falter in subsequent years.
- All students must be continually monitored to assure they are making progress, reading books at the right level for learning, and not suffering from any gaps in their knowledge. Teachers can best accomplish this by taking observational notes while the student reads.
- Children need to learn the skills beyond phonics, phonemic awareness and word-attack strategies which extend reading.

These include spelling, grammar, word and language structures, and mechanics. (p. 283)

In summary, for these children to reach their reading potential in the later grades, early, direct assistance in the alphabetic and language system must be provided.

Myth #2: Organized, Explicit Phonics Programs Result in Rigid Pedagogy

The second argument advanced by whole-language advocates is that all too often phonics programs are taught in a sterile, lock-step manner using worksheets with low-level activities. These activities are not related to the particular needs of the student and offer little practice in using and learning skills in the context of reading materials that actually reinforced the skills lessons. *This criticism is correct, and such ineffective implementation strategies should be avoided.*

The phonemic and phonics strands that are being advocated as part of a balanced approach by our top practitioners and reading experts are designed to be (a) directly taught by teachers; (b) presented in an active, problem-solving manner that develops conscious understanding of the sound/symbol system; (c) tailored much more precisely to the specific needs of children; and (d) taught by providing students with numerous opportunities to use and practice the skills in the context of reading.

Successful Early Reading Programs in Practice

The most effective teachers are *already* using the best practices proposed by the advocates of a balanced approach. A recent study of teachers nominated as the most effective in teaching children to read, most of whom considered themselves whole-language teachers, showed that these skilled practitioners provide the rich array of whole-language activities described above (Pressley & Rankin, 1994). However, they also are concerned that their children learn phonics.

These effective teachers explicitly teach the following:

- Phonemic awareness
- Visual discrimination
- Letter-sound relationships
- The alphabetic principle that letters and letter patterns need to be distinguished, since they stand for different sounds
- Decoding and word-attack skills (pp. 163-164)

For the most part, these experienced professionals teach these skills by having students read appropriate materials, but they also teach the skills in isolation, usually in relatively small blocks of time, in a problem-solving, active manner with the aim of giving students conscious control of the sound/symbol system. Skills teaching is especially prevalent for weaker readers and in special education. These excellent teachers are able to use and integrate a number of complicated instructional strategies to tailor effective approaches for the diverse needs of their students. It has taken most of them years of effort, study, and commitment to reach this level of effectiveness.

Essential Components of an Effective Literacy Strategy

During the past two decades, cognitive scientists and the country's top reading experts have corroborated the effectiveness of what our best practitioners have been doing all along. Their research has produced a much clearer picture of the essential components and instructional strategies of an effective early literacy program.

The consensus of these reading experts is that an effective literacy program for all children must include *both* a multitude of print and language-rich (whole language) activities such as reading to children, discussing stories, and writing frequently *and* explicit, organized, and systematic skills development.

These top experts agree that the goals of any early reading program should be to enable almost every student to comprehend and read fluently grade-appropriate material, understand the meaning of what they have read, be well-read, and enjoy and be able to learn from reading.

These specialists also maintain that these goals can be accomplished only if most students are independently reading beginning books by mid-first grade (or the equivalent in ungraded primaries).

For early reading to occur, *children first need to learn the technical skills that enable them to read:* awareness of the sound structure of words, the system of letter/sound correspondences, and word-attack and other self-teaching techniques—especially the ability to generate plausible alternative pronunciations for letter patterns and then resolve the ambiguity through the meaning of the passage (e.g., the first reading of *bread*). They *also* need to be provided with opportunities to practice these skills in reading and writing words and stories.

This skills development strand should be *sequenced and adjusted individually* if a student already knows the skill, *and* it must include *large amounts of practice,* both to develop automaticity with a growing number of words and to become more adept at decoding new words until the use of these skills becomes automatic. Students should be taught to understand the components, relationships, and overall structure of the sound/symbol system.

Skills should be taught *explicitly and directly,* not as rote learning, but in an *active, thinking, problem-solving way* (children as "word detectives"), with the reading of interesting stories and nonfiction materials as the medium for learning to use and think about these skills. This can be accomplished by reading with the teacher in guided practice, reading with a classmate or a parent, reading along with a taped version of the story, or just by reading independently. Initially, these materials should be either specifically designed or appropriate to reinforce the skills being learned.

Finally, the experts recommend that for students to become readers by mid-first grade, the following sequence of benchmarks and instruction should be adopted.

1. Students must leave *kindergarten* knowing letter names, shapes and some letter sounds; possessing basic phonemic, syntactic, and print awareness; and having listening, discussion, and oral telling and retelling skills.

2. *During the first 4 months of first grade,* students must learn basic sound/symbol system correspondences, more advanced phonemic and syntactic awareness, blending and word-attack strategic skills, automatic recognition of basic high-frequency words and word families, comprehension skills, and how to

use these tools in combination to read for meaning. Writing or spelling out words (especially the words they are reading), which necessitates encoding sounds into letter patterns, is also one of the best ways to learn phonics.

Thus, by mid-first grade, most children should have learned the critical mass of skills that enable them to begin reading books or anthologies, *including both literature and nonfiction at appropriate levels of difficulty.* These materials then become the vehicle to learn and apply the skills being taught in specific lessons. By this stage, many students should be increasingly able to teach themselves and learn the rest of the letter/sound system by reading large amounts of material. These independent learners still should be taught more advanced decoding skills, be taught to recognize an increasing number of words automatically by reading specific words successfully several times, and be monitored for progress and gaps in learning by the teacher. However, many children who have auditory or visual processing problems or who have very little exposure to reading and reading materials will need more structured lessons in these beginning-reading techniques well into the second and third grades.

Consequently, from mid-first grade on, a balanced program should extend reading power. It should provide *extensive opportunities for students to read varied books and materials;* offer explicit instruction in comprehension and oral language development; and teach other skills strands such as spelling, the more complex syllabication patterns, word and language structure, grammar, composition, vocabulary and mechanics.

If schools follow these guidelines, almost every child should become a strong reader.

Comprehensive and Balanced:
Not the Same as Eclectic

Contrary to what some critics may think, a balanced approach does not mean a mushy eclecticism. Beginning-to-read strategies must incorporate a set of strands that is comprehensive enough to assure all children will read. Within this set, each strand must be designed according to best practices and be thoughtfully integrated and reinforced by other strands.

However, these symbol/sound skill-strands must not become so jumbled with other strands that students miss the point, as is currently the case with much classroom instruction that stresses integrated language arts activities and attempts to deal with skills on the fly or haphazardly. Nor should skills be taught in such an isolated and rote manner that students fail to connect skill understanding with the actual practice of reading.

These beginning-to-read strategies are consistent with the English/ Language Arts performance standards being developed by the New Standards Project, a national standards-setting effort supported by states representing more than half the students in the nation. These performance standards require students to be

- Fluent readers by the fourth grade
- Well-read
- Able to understand grade-level materials
- Able to apply their writing skills to organize information
- Able to argue a point, tell a story, and respond to a literary or nonfiction piece
- Able to participate in an ongoing conversation or make a more formal presentation to the class
- Proficient in spelling, grammar, and language mechanics
- Able to effectively discuss the ideas contained in literature or nonfiction

These strategies also are consistent with the California English/ Language Arts Framework, a K-12 document written in the late 1980s, which makes important points about the need for literature-rich classrooms and an integrated language arts program; the necessity of being well-read; the potency of literature; and the importance of the ability to understand and discuss ideas. *However, although it does state that phonics and skills are important, it is neither specific enough nor clear enough about the essential beginning-to-read strategies for preschool, kindergarten, and early primary grades.* Consequently, as most people involved in education now realize, the framework needs to be supplemented in these areas. The recently released report of the California Reading Task Force (1995), "Every Child a Reader," confirms the need for organized, explicit skills strands as an important part of a comprehensive reading program.

SUMMARY

According to the overwhelming consensus of the best practitioners and top researchers, an effective reading program should be integrated with the other language arts such as writing, speaking, and listening. High-quality early literacy programs also should include many of the activities now characterized as "whole language," which aim to create a print- and language-rich environment through reading aloud to students and discussing literature and nonfiction with children; a strong independent-reading strand based on the availability of good children's literature; writing to communicate; and many shared reading activities.

However, because these instructional strategies are, by themselves, not enough to teach many children to read well, specific skills development components also must be included, such as phonemic awareness (the ability to hear segments of sounds in spoken language and consciously manipulate them), phonics (letter/sound correspondences), print awareness, word structure, and word-attack and self-monitoring skills. In addition, these skills must be taught in an organized and systematic manner at the beginning of any reading program if all children are going to learn to read. Students should be taught these skills in an active, problem-solving manner that offers plenty of opportunities to practice the skills in actual reading and writing situations.

Chapters 3 through 8 address the recommended specific components of an organized skills program, when these skills should be taught, and how they should be taught. A timeline that summarizes the reading skills curriculum is included in Appendix B.

Notes

1. For a penetrating attack on this naturalistic fallacy, see Pressley and Rankin (1994), pp. 160-161. These authors find that the original research done by Chomsky, who assumed that oral language syntactical competence cannot be taught, has not held up. Most special education programs now do successfully teach language structure. In addition, the mental processes used for reading such as visual processing, visual discrimination, visual short-term memory, and phonological awareness evolved in humans for very different purposes than reading and writing and need assistance to be converted to the complicated task of deciphering print, whereas a case can be made that oral

processing abilities did evolve to assist humans in understanding and producing speech and operate much more automatically.

2. For an excellent explanation of how the ability to learn to speak depends on the recognition of deep patterns that are biologically hard-wired in our brains (in contrast to learning to read) see Steven Pinker's 1994 best-seller, *The Language Instinct: How the Mind Creates Language.*

3. Some of the most comprehensive research on this issue that supports the necessity for a structured skills component has been directed and sponsored by Dr. G. Reid Lyon of the National Institute of Child, Health, and Human Development in Bethesda, Maryland. This institute has invested more than $80 million in large-scale research projects and longitudinal studies of children during the past several years to ascertain the causes of learning disabilities and determine if the consensus position on a balanced approach to teaching beginning reading is correct. This research is described by Lyon in *Research in Learning Disabilities at the NICHD* (1994) and "Research Initiatives in Learning Disabilities" (1995). The former document cites findings from the sponsored research projects that have studied these issues and conducted intensive longitudinal studies of large numbers of students from early childhood to high school. Some of their findings: "Reading disabled or dyslexic children comprise 20% of students and three quarters of third-grade students who are reading disabled will remain disabled in the ninth grade" (p. 10). "Disabled readers do not readily acquire the alphabetic code when learning to read due to deficiencies in phonological processing. As such, disabled readers must be presented highly structured, explicit and intensive instruction in phonics rules and the application of the rules to print" (p. 12). "The ability to read and comprehend depends upon rapid and automatic recognition and decoding of single words and slow and inaccurate decoding are the best predictors of difficulty in reading comprehension" (p. 11). "The ability to decode single words accurately and fluently is dependent upon the ability to segment words and syllables into abstract constituent sound unites (phonemes). Deficits in phonological awareness reflect the core deficit in dyslexia" (p. 10). "The best predictor of reading ability/disability from kindergarten and first grade test performance is phoneme segmentation ability" (p. 11). "Longitudinal data indicate that systematic structured phonics instruction results in more favorable outcomes in reading that does a context-emphasis (whole language) approach" (p. 12).

4. Lyon (1995) writes that "[r]eading disability reflects a persistent deficit rather than a development lag in linguistic and reading skills [citations omitted]" (p. 10). Resistance to early instruction in preschool, kindergarten, and early first grade sometimes stems from a confusion of two meanings of "developmentally appropriate." The more hard-line *maturational* approach states that students are not ready for instruction and need "the gift of time." Lyon's research and other studies demonstrate that only a very small number of students cannot master the skills being discussed for kindergarten and first grade, such as letter recognition, sound blending, and beginning phonics. It is not "developmentally appropriate" to wait. A more realistic interventionist approach maintains that organized instructional support (which can be game-

like) at the appropriate time is beneficial. The research cited above goes further and finds intervention is essential. For most students at risk of not learning to read, the failure to intervene early means they will never become proficient readers.

2

What Skilled Readers Do

What is it about learning to read that makes the skills of hearing the sounds of written words, decoding, and word attack so important? To understand the importance of these skills to beginning readers, it is first necessary to examine the nature of *skilled* reading and then a different and more complex issue—the process of learning to read.

The Importance of
Seeing Letter Combinations in Words

A few essentials about reading will ground the following section. One of the best discussions of this topic is found in *Beginning to Read,* Marilyn Adams's comprehensive 1990 review of how children learn to read. The book's foreword was written by David Pearson, who codirected the Center for the Study of Reading at the University of Illinois that produced *On Becoming a Nation of Readers* in the early 1980s and greatly influenced the California English/Language Arts framework. In the foreword, he explains how the book stemmed from work done in response to a U.S. Office of Education Research Institute request to review all aspects of phonics and early reading instruction in a straightforward and evenhanded way. The Center had been investigating comprehension research, and, according to Pearson, Adams was the natural candidate to summarize the breakthroughs made in research during the '80s about the history of the English alphabet; the controversies surrounding phonics instruction; issues and research in early reading instruction; basic perceptual and reading processes; and the processes involved in identifying sounds, letters, words, and meaning.

In her book, Adams makes the essential point that although reading is a meaning-driven activity and the production of independent readers capable of understanding meaning is a goal of reading instruction, *the key to unlocking meaning for proficient readers starts with the automatic recognition of **each single written word**. The recognition of a word is accomplished by extremely rapid, accurate, and complete visual recognition of letters and patterns of letters in that word which then initiates the mind to search for an accurate match with a word stored in long-term memory.* This search is reinforced and accelerated by clues stemming from the meaning and language structure of what is being read and, when necessary, by hearing the word mentally and determining if the prospective candidate word match makes sense. These secondary mental systems operate simultaneously and in tandem with the spelling pattern scanning, until the meaning of that word is retrieved from long-term memory and becomes conscious.

The automatic recognition of words frees a student's mind to concentrate on the meaning of the word in relation to its phrase, the sentence, and the story. For proficient readers, automatic recognition takes place swiftly, effortlessly, and unconsciously, and uses a minimum of working memory capacity, allowing the reader to concentrate on the meaning of the passage (Adams, 1990, pp. 107-135; Juel, 1994, pp. 1-2). Share and Stanovich (1995b) write that "there is no known teaching method that has resulted in good reading comprehension without simultaneously leading to the development of at least adequate word recognition ability. Furthermore, an overwhelming amount of evidence indicates that the proximal impediment to reading in at-risk and reading-disabled children is difficulty in recognizing words [citations omitted]" (p. 3).

The Mental
Mechanisms of Reading Proficiency

Adams (1990) labels the mental structure that recognizes letters and letter patterns in words as the *orthographic* (spelling) *processor.* This process of recognizing words by the letter patterns works only if the reader has good command of two other critical mental systems: one dealing with connecting print to sounds, the other using the structure and meaning of the passage to accelerate the search process. The first is called the *phonological processor.* It is defined as the ability to mentally represent the system of sounds underlying spoken words, perceive their relationship to letter patterns, and use that knowledge to search for the potential sounds associated with those particular letter patterns as assistance in finding the right word stored in memory.[1] The second system is called a *context and meaning processor.* This involves the ability to break the text into phrases and clauses that constitute natural (syntactical) chunks of text.

This "chunking" facilitates retention of the meaning of strings of words in the reader's mind. At the same time, it provides the reader with hints about whether any of the potential word candidates being generated from memory by the letter and sound clues make sense in relation to the meaning of what is being read (Adams, 1990).[2] These two backup mental systems—perceiving sound and testing for meaning—operate simultaneously, when needed, with the visual recognition of letter patterns, thus speeding up the recognition process.

All three mental abilities interact with each other as often as necessary to narrow down the candidate words stored in memory that could possibly match the letter patterns and potential associated sounds while also being consistent with the meaning of the passage, until the exact appropriate match is found and becomes conscious. The entire process is automatic, unconscious, extremely rapid, and perceived by the accomplished reader as effortless. The reader is busy attending to the meaning of the word just retrieved in relation to other words and phrases that have already been read.

There are several widespread misconceptions about how skilled readers actually read. For example, it is commonly believed that skilled readers do not need to read letters or even words because that would slow them down. But according to extensive eye movement research, even accomplished readers *do look at virtually every word, although they sometimes skip short function words such as* and, to, the, *or* of.

They accurately perceive every letter in those words, not linearly, but in chunks (Adams, 1990, pp. 100-102). They do this so rapidly—averaging five words or more per second—that they can recognize phrases and words at almost the same time they recognize individual letters.

This seeming paradox can be explained. Skilled readers, although they perceive every letter, do not need to see each one independently; rather, they can simultaneously search both the print and their long-term memories for matching patterns. Thus they look at letters in combination, and because they have so much prior experience with the variety of high-frequency letter or spelling patterns in words and how words are broken into syllables, they can quickly use this knowledge to narrow down the possibilities and find the word that exactly fits a particular pattern (Adams, 1990, pp. 108-115).

Here is what happens mentally. Readers who see a *t* followed by an *h* unconsciously know that a high probability sequence in English is *th,* and they therefore more quickly process both the *t* and the *h*. If the word being decoded is *therefore,* skilled readers simultaneously break the word into two syllables; see highly associated patterns of *th, ere,* or *there* to quickly match with the word *there;* do the same with *fore;* unconsciously determine that there is not a pattern of *ref* or *refore;* and then locate a match with the word *therefore* in their long-term memory. At the same time, the phonological mental structure is checking out possible sounds for these various combinations through its knowledge of the most likely sounds for the potential letter combinations being analyzed, helping to narrow and confirm the direction of the search. When all systems agree, the word becomes conscious (Adams, 1990; Ehri, 1994, in press; Juel, 1994; Share & Stanovich, 1995b).[3]

Thus it is apparent why another misconception about reading is detrimental. Beginning readers who rely too heavily on contextual clues, such as pictures or the connection of other words in the passage, are distracted from looking at the letters in a word and connecting those letter patterns to words in their minds. Contextual and structural clues do accelerate reading in proficient readers but cannot replace looking at letter patterns to initiate the mental search for a word. According to Andrew Biemiller (1994), a noted researcher from the University of Toronto, proficient sixth-grade readers can recognize words about .20 to .25 seconds faster if words are read in context rather than out of context, effectively doubling their reading speed from approximately ½ second a word to ¼ second a word, or 240 words per minute. Biemiller is also critical of claims that children can learn to read relying on context clues without learning the alphabetic principle and the sound/symbol system. Moreover, Biemiller underscores that becoming proficient in reading requires graphophonic ability and that even proficient readers revert to a graphophonic reading strategy when confronted with difficult material or with words they do not know. Logically, then, readers should be encouraged to try to read every word and to look at the letters in each word if they wish to read fluently. Even when students ask for assistance with a word, they should subsequently try to read it (pp. 203-209).

A final strategy presented by some advocates—and one still widely practiced in many classrooms—is having children try to read by looking at the shape or configuration of the word. This is an extremely inefficient strategy. It is the scanning of the *letter patterns* in a word that starts the processes which unlock meaning in proficient readers (Adams, 1990, pp. 96-97). Again, balance is the key. Reliance on contextual clues is a technique usually used by readers with poor decoding skills and correlates with low reading performance (Share & Stanovich, 1995b, pp. 5-6). Conversely, word calling—saying the word without apparent understanding of meaning—can be evidence of weak meaning or syntactical cueing systems, since these are also associated with low reading levels (Pinnell, Pikulski et al., 1995, p. 22). However, often what appears to be word calling is, in fact, a slowing down caused by weak decoding skills and difficult material (Share & Stanovich, 1995b).[4]

Skills Needed to
Become a Proficient Reader

Research showing what good readers do helps focus the discussion but does not necessarily answer the question of how a person *becomes* a skilled reader—that is a different story. For example, knowing how to sound out a word may be essential as a way station to effortless recognition of that word; phonics helps a student read a new word or place that word in long-term memory by forcing the mind to attend to spelling and sound patterns. However, sounding out words is a very slow and cumbersome process, and any student who must rely on sounding out in order to read many words is not reading fluently enough to concentrate on meaning.

How do children learn to become fluent readers? Which skills and mental abilities are most important and in what order? What sequence do the best practitioners and reading experts recommend? What should be taught in the skills-development strand, when should it be learned, and how does it fit with other language-arts strands?

Adams (1990, 1991, 1995), Juel and Beck (1995), Pearson (1993), Share (1995), Stanovich (1986, 1993), and almost all other reading experts maintain that children need explicit instruction in phonemic awareness, decoding, print awareness, word-attack skills, and language structure, including phrasing, syllabic, word root, and spelling patterns—all with sufficient repetition and reinforcement so that they can learn to recognize large numbers of words automatically and decode new words efficiently. Only then will children be able to read fluently and thus be able to concentrate on meaning. It is also crucial that students develop sufficient reading proficiency at an early age, so that they can use reading large amounts of text as a key method of developing fluency.

What is it about these skills that makes them so important in becoming fluent? It is important to underscore that none of these experts advocates that these component skills be the *only* strands in a reading or language arts program or that they should be taught in complete isolation from the act of reading connected text. Right from the start, children should see the purpose of reading, become instilled with a love of reading and books, think about the ideas or beauty of stories, and engage in a multitude of oral- and written-language activities. But for many children, these activities cannot replace a separate but connected age-appropriate and individually appropriate skills development component in preschool, kindergarten, and early first grade. This is what enables them to *start* reading in first grade. Subsequent skills-development strands will extend their reading and decoding skills and assist them in becoming independent learners.

To understand what beginners need to do to learn to read, it is helpful to understand why some children have difficulty learning to read. One of the biggest obstacles to word recognition, and thus to print comprehension among less skilled readers, both in terms of automatically recognizing growing numbers of words and deciphering new words, is difficulty in decoding, that is, turning spellings into sounds (Pressley & Cariglia-Bull, 1995, pp. 30-31). Share and Stanovich (1995b) write that "We know unequivocally that less-skilled readers have difficulty turning spellings into sounds. . . . This relationship is so strong that it deserves to be identified as one, if not the defining feature of reading disability [citations omitted]" (p. 7). Children have difficulty learning this skill in early first grade if they have not sufficiently developed the ability to become aware of and manipulate the discrete sound segments that comprise words (phonemic awareness) (Adams, 1990, pp. 293-332; Juel, 1994, p. 4; Pressley & Cariglia-Bull, 1995, p. 24; Share & Stanovich, 1995b, pp. 9-10) and if they have not learned enough of the letter/sound correspondence system and word-attack strategies—such as sounding out, recognizing similar letter/sound patterns or generating alternative pronunciations for given letter patterns (phonics or decoding) to be able to teach themselves the complete system of letter/sound patterns through extensive reading (Adams, 1990, pp. 293-332; Pressley & Cariglia-Bull, 1995, pp. 30-31; Share, p. 191).[5] Extensive reading should start in mid-first grade, but this ability depends on learning decoding in early first grade, which in turn depends on reaching basic levels of phonemic awareness by the end of kindergarten.

As we shall see, these two overarching abilities—phonemic awareness and decoding—are mutually dependent and reinforcing. A child cannot learn decoding without phonemic awareness, and the process of connecting letters to the pronunciations of and sounds in words is one of the best ways of learning to segment sounds.

Notes

1. According to Adams (1990), the phonological processor feeds back the sounds that various orders of letters and words make to the visual processing and associations occurring in the orthographic processor. This processor accelerates the visual recognition of letter patterns by adding the sound patterns of words to help rule out unlikely words or letter combinations or point to probable combinations. It also helps decipher new words or complex spelling patterns if they follow recognizable sequences. As Adams explains,

> The phonological processor helps in one other task of comprehension. Comprehension is a two-stage process. First, the reader identifies each successive word and its appropriate meaning as defined by its immediate context. Secondly, the reader interprets the entire string of words just read, considering the relations among the just-read words to each other as well as to any background knowledge and larger understanding of the text that can be brought to bear.

Translating the string of words just decoded into sound (recoding) and keeping them in short term memory while the next word is visually processed can help resolve ambiguities in the word or help narrow meaning choices. For a continuing, sensible interpretation, the following two conditions must exist:

The grouping must be recognizable clauses or sentences or, in technical terms, at major syntactic boundaries. Otherwise, the string of words to be compiled will be syntactically incomplete and " . . . make no sense." The performance of skilled readers indicates that they generally prefer to recode at the boundaries between sentences or whole clauses. In keeping with this, when skilled readers are in the course of reading a clause, their ability to recall its precise wording is extremely rapid and accurate. In contrast, the fine, verbatim memory for the clause is all but lost just as soon as they start reading the next.

Skilled readers characteristically pause at the end of major syntactic units to wrap-up and assure themselves that everything is making sense; if the interpretation of the just-read clause requires inference or complicated pronoun references, the wrap-up is significantly increased. In summary, for this wrap-up to work, it is also important that the reader has a complete and ordered memory and the phonological processor assists in that task. (p. 186)

2. Adams explains that the meaning and context processor continually feeds information to the visual processing of letter patterns (and to the phonological processor) to (1) both screen out unlikely meanings of words and point to likely ones based on both accumulated knowledge of the connection of word meanings and letter patterns, and (2) point to the most likely meaning of a word because of the meaning of the string of words it is in.

3. There is still some controversy over whether and how much the phonological back-up system needs to be activated when a word such as *girl* or *and* has been read so many times that the spelling pattern of the whole word has become memorized and automatic. Although Adams (1990, p. 104) claims that skilled readers do mentally "hear" the pronunciations of the words they read (called recoding), the weight of the research community seems to support the proposition that a skilled reader can unconsciously directly access a word by just looking at the spelling without mentally recoding it—thus speeding up the reading process considerably. In this view, memorized words can be read unmediated by the sound/letter system once they have been read so often that they become automatic.

Researchers strongly insist, however, that recoding or connecting the letter patterns to the word's sounds is an essential step the first times a word is read until the spelling pathways are established in the mind. That is why decoding ability and phonemic awareness are so essential in learning to read.

4. According to Share and Stanovich (1995b), "The failure to take into account the interaction between the difficulty of materials and readers skill . . . leads to a misinterpretation of the frequent reports from teachers of children who 'just plod through and don't use context.' These reports usually turn out to be spurious, not because they are untrue, but because the common interpretation—that the children are plodding (recognizing words slowly) *because* they are not using context—is false. The research reviewed above leads to just the opposite conclusion: the children are not using context because they are plodding, e.g., decoding inefficiently. Given texts of equal functional difficulty, good readers would also 'plod' [citations omitted]" (p. 6).

5. According to Share (1995), "Reliable and substantial gains in reading ability have been consistently obtained in both laboratory and field settings when *both* phonemic awareness *and* symbol-sound correspondences have been trained [citations omitted]. Since training studies tend to show that neither letter-sound knowledge alone [citations omitted], nor phonemic awareness alone [citations omitted] are sufficient, we can conclude that phonemic awareness (in conjunction with lettersound knowledge) is a causal *co-requisite* for successful reading acquisition" (p. 191).

3

Beginning-to-Read
Instruction for Preschool
and Kindergarten

Students need specific prereading skills in order to learn to read
on schedule. Unfortunately, many students are not acquiring
these skills early enough to profit by first-grade literacy instruction.
George Farkus (personal communication, April 1995), a University of
Texas researcher who runs a successful tutoring program with the
Dallas school system, has found that 85% of students graduating from
Dallas kindergartens do not know the names of the letters, cannot
recognize their shapes, and possess only rudimentary knowledge of
the sounds they represent. *Yet, a strong finding of research is that one
of the best predictors of first-grade reading ability is the fast and
accurate skill of naming and recognizing the shapes of letters* (Adams,
1990, p. 61).[1]

Listening to Stories, Discussing Them,
and Oral Expression—at School and at Home

This chapter discusses the skills strands that should be taught before first grade. Preliminarily, it is important to reiterate that these skills should be taught in combination with regularly occurring rich oral language activities: reading good stories and informational texts to children and then discussing them; having students tell and retell stories; listening to, reciting, or singing nursery rhymes or songs, including the Alphabet Song; pretend reading, picture reading, and shared reading; playing with magnetic letters; discussing word meaning and group and individual story writing.[2]

According to David Dickinson (1994), one of the key elements distinguishing effective preschools and kindergartens from less effective ones is the nature of teacher-student talk. The more effective teachers use discussions about books, behavior, or even giving directions as opportunities for encouraging children to think, predict, extend, or make personal connections. Vocabulary analysis is also important. This analytic talk can be as simple as asking children to give the reasons for a rule or tell how one story is like another (this strategy works for parents, too). These teachers use the technique judiciously; not all conversation needs to be this challenging, but enough stretching is encouraged to make a huge difference in performance.

Dickinson found that a more didactic approach—one in which discussions of readings involved low-level recall questions, little talk before or after the story, and limited amounts of teacher and student talk during readings—was less effective. Similarly, too much teacher-student talk during readings (students continually being asked to clarify and amplify meanings) detracted from student engagement and understanding. The best approach was what Dickinson labels a performance-oriented approach, characterized by large amounts of teacher and student talk before and after the readings, such as questions connecting the story to favorite books or individual experiences. Questions during the story were limited to spontaneous analytical responses involving predictions, personal connections, and vocabulary analysis.

On the home front, Pressley and Cariglia-Bull (1995) describe how the home environment is also a major potential contributor to emergent literacy. In a literacy-nurturing environment, there are rich family conversations, ready availability of a variety of reading and writing materials and plastic letters, and parents who hold a high positive regard for literacy for themselves and their children. Such parents read to their children extensively, ask analytic questions, and value reading. Books are ubiquitous in the home, parents take children to libraries and bookstores, and television is limited. Parents can be taught successfully how to ask more analytical questions, that is, open-ended or about the attributes or functions of objects in stories (Pressley & Cariglia-Bull, 1995, p. 22).

Naming and Recognizing Letters

According to Marilyn Adams's exhaustive review of the research (Adams, 1990, pp. 341-364), learning to name and accurately recognize letters is a crucial first step to reading for the following reasons:

- A child who can recognize most letters with thorough confidence will have an easier time learning about letter sounds and word spellings than a child who also has to work at distinguishing the individual letters.
- Automatic, accurate recognition of letters as wholes frees mental energy to concentrate on recognizing patterns of letters—a key to reading.
- In general, because the names of most letters are closely associated with their sounds, children who learn to name letters also begin learning their sounds. More importantly, they learn to grasp what is probably the single most important understanding enabling children to learn how to read: the alphabetic principle that letters have corresponding sounds that make words when combined. (Adams, 1990, pp. 63-64)

Teaching Letter Recognition

Adams recommends that the best way to learn letters is first to concentrate on learning the names of letters, then to learn to recognize their corresponding shapes, and finally, to establish the concept of letter/sound correspondences. Note that this strategy is *not* to have children learn the names of letters by showing them the letters; this is backward. Children first learn the names through devices such as the

Alphabet Song (usually before school) or by associating a letter with its name and then learning to recognize the shape associated with that name. This latter process takes much longer and is complicated by the confusing similarities in letter shape, such as *d* and *b*. Longitudinal studies consistently have indicated that the learning of letter names comes well before the learning of their sounds. Typically children can recite the alphabet before age 4,[3] but need up to 2 years to learn the corresponding shapes.

Knowing names and shapes of letters protects children from becoming confused when they learn the sounds and ensures that students will know that the letter names are in fact names. Since the phonological processor is helped by rhyme, rhythm, and pitch, songs are particularly effective ways of learning. This name/shape strategy— used in the Alphabet Song and ABC books—has proved its worth over the years and is supported and reinforced by parents who shared the same experiences. Additionally, the name of the letter usually is an important clue to at least one of the sounds of the letter.

Finally, and of great importance, research shows that learning to identify and name letters frequently turns into interest in their sounds and in the spelling of words. Adams (1990) cites research that also shows that knowing letter names is strongly correlated with both the ability to remember the forms of written words and the tendency to treat them as ordered sequences of letters rather than holistic patterns. Conversely, the research also shows that *not* knowing letter names is coupled with extreme difficulty in learning letter sounds and word recognition.

Marilyn Adams (1990) urges that instruction in letter recognition start long before children arrive at first grade so that they are highly familiar with letter shapes before they are faced with the tasks of learning the letters' sounds or learning to read words. These tasks begin in earnest in the early first grade. Use of magnetic letters and games; the presence of classroom labels; recognition of each other's names; attention to signs; and reading, writing, and singing activities help with the task of learning to recognize letter shapes. During kindergarten, there should be an organized effort (some combination of letter play and direct teaching) to assure that students learn most of the letters and their shapes in both upper and lower case and a few letter sounds. According to Adams (1990), "Learning to recognize and discriminate printed letters is just too big, too hard, and too fussy a task to be mastered incidentally, in tandem with some other hard and fussy task, or without an adult's focused attention to its progress and difficulties. . . . [W]hat a waste to correct the pronunciation of a letter sound or word if the child's confusion was really in the visual identity of the letter" (p. 363).

Writing the Letters/First Words

A complementary strategy for learning individual letters is to practice writing them. Having children learn to write the letters accurately, especially with encouragement to attend to their distinctive features, significantly helps letter recognition. Kindergartners also can begin to write some easy words. Many programs categorize letter shapes or establish motor patterns for each letter as an aid to this process. Copying, and especially tracing, are not as useful in teaching the recognition of individual letter shapes because students do not necessarily have to pay attention to either the letter's sound or its name, much less to its distinctive differences from other letters (Adams, 1990, p. 355; Clay, 1993, pp. 24-27).

The Importance of Phonemic Awareness

According to the latest research, the best predictor of reading success is whether the child has developed basic phonemic or phonological awareness—the ability to consciously pick out and manipulate from spoken words the smallest sound chunks that make up those words. These chunks are called **phonemes.** They usually are smaller sound segments than syllables (Adams, 1990, p. 65; Cunningham, 1990; Juel, 1994, pp. 4, 16-17; Liberman et al., 1991, p. 12; Share & Stanovich, 1995b, pp. 9-10; Torgesen & Hecht, in press).

Because speech is heard naturally as a continuous stream of sound, and short words and syllables are heard as one sound, preliterate individuals—whether they are children or adults—must be taught how to segment these sound chunks. For example, children and adults hear the word *bag* as a whole, even though it is made up of three phonemes.

Well-developed phonemic awareness is not just the ability to hear phonemes, to discriminate between two phonemes, or even to produce them. It is the ability to be conscious of these sound segments and to be able to manipulate them on demand. It took humans tens or hundreds of thousands of years to develop language. Every human language has the unique ability to combine a finite number of sounds to generate a huge number of words. In contrast, nonlanguage symbolic systems such as traffic signs can never have more than a few symbols.

These sound chunks are interchangeable parts, but they follow rules of combination. Humans have evolved so they can easily intuit these rules. An infant becomes a speaker of the language he or she is born into, learning how to say phonemes and combine them into words according to what is acceptable in that language. This process happens unconsciously and, for the most part, automatically. Almost every human being achieves fluency in oral language (Pinker, 1994).

Ironically, that very oral fluency is an obstacle to learning to read. Children have become so automatic and swift at hearing discrete sounds as whole by overlapping the sounds that they must relearn how to break up the word into its constituent sound segments. Students must become aware of how sounds generate words—the deep phonological principle behind all language, and organize that system in their long-term memory if they are to decipher an alphabetic script. In Adams's (1990) words, "To learn an alphabetic script, we must learn to attend to that which we learned not to attend to" (p. 66).

To summarize, phonemic awareness is the ability to understand consciously and analytically that words are made up of sound segments that are abstract and can be manipulated. It depends on installing that system in long-term memory and having it available to working memory when deciphering a printed word. Use of phonological knowledge is an essential prerequisite to the process of connecting the letters and patterns of letters in writing to words stored in the memory (Adams, 1990, p. 65). For those who have not reached a level of phonemic awareness that enables them to profit from phonics instruction in the early grades, it must be taught or 90% of these children will fail to learn to read in first grade and will never recover (Blachman, 1991).[4] Isabelle and Alvin Liberman, respected researchers in this field, estimated that 30% of students they sampled did not understand the internal phonemic structure of words even at the end of a full year of school. In their opinion, almost every poor reader has a very weak understanding of this phonological structure (Liberman, Shankweiler, & Liberman, 1991; see also Adams, 1990, p. 293 et seq.; Juel, 1994, pp. 1-24; Lundberg, 1991).

Some whole-language advocates have argued that since children all learn to speak effortlessly without being taught, they should learn to read just as easily—the naturalist fallacy. The English written language is based on an amazing human invention, the alphabetic principle, which stems from the insight that words have an internal structure and can be broken into sound chunks that then can be represented by letters and combinations of letters to constitute written words. Many sophisticated cultures never developed a writing system based on this alphabetic system. To expect children to discover on their own what a few unsung geniuses figured out very recently in our species' history is hopelessly romantic. The vast findings of the scientific and research communities refute the proposition that most children can accomplish this task unaided (Share & Stanovich, 1995b, pp. 31-32). In fact, these findings strongly indicate just the opposite: Most children need help in developing phonemic awareness before they can map letters and letter combinations to spoken words and map language onto the printed page (Pressley & Rankin, 1994, p. 161). In contrast, children are genetically predisposed to learn how to speak and understand language without much adult assistance (Pinker, 1994).

Numerous research studies of nonliterate peoples, nonreaders, and children before they learn to read—all of whom have great difficulty in segmenting spoken words into phonemes—have confirmed these findings. These findings also have been confirmed in studies of children born with profound hearing deficiencies, who have never heard language. Many of these children will read significantly below grade level. The ones who do reach high levels of reading proficiency have invariably figured out the phonological principle by alternative methods such as oral training, lip-reading, or seeing spelling patterns (Liberman et al., 1991, pp. 21-22).

Teaching Phonemic Awareness

According to Marilyn Adams (1990), there are five levels of phonemic awareness, the first four of which should be reached by the end of kindergarten.

1. *The ability to hear rhymes and alliteration as measured by knowledge of nursery rhymes.* This is the most primitive level.
2. *The ability to do oddity tasks* (which first sound is different in the oral words *pig, hill,* and *pin?;* which last sound is different in *doll, hop,* and *top?;* or which middle sound is different in words such as

pin, gun, bun?). This ability requires the child to compare and contrast the sounds of words for rhyme or alliteration and rests on the ability to focus attention not just on the sounds of words but on the components of their sounds that make them similar or different.

3. *The abilities to blend orally* (what word do the sounds /m/, /a/, and /p/ make?) *and split syllables* (i.e., break off the first phoneme—the instructor says *bear* and students say *b-b-b,* or last phoneme—the instructor says *pink* and students say *ink*). This requires subdividing words into those small, meaningless sounds corresponding to phonemes; the ability to recognize the way phonemes sound when produced "in isolation"; and, better yet, the ability to produce phonemes that way by oneself. (David Share (1995) argues that phonemic blending is the key phonemic awareness ability in learning to read [pp. 193-194].)

4. *The ability to perform phonemic segmentation*—tapping out with a stick or using counters to represent the number of phonemes heard in words or syllables with one, two, or three phonemes (three taps for the word *mat*). This level of phonemic awareness first requires the ability to understand that a word can be completely analyzed into a series of phonemes and to analyze them completely when asked. The next stage of phonemic segmentation is the ability to match a plastic letter or letter tile with the sounds in words. This ability should develop during late kindergarten.

5. *The ability to perform phoneme manipulation tasks* (say *hill* without the *h*). These tasks require sufficient proficiency with the phonemic structure of words that students are able to add, delete, or move any designated phoneme and eventually multisyllabic units, and then regenerate a word or nonwords from the result. This level is appropriate for middle to late first grade (Adams, 1990, p. 80).

Phonemic Awareness Activities

Every kindergarten program should aim at assuring that students enter first grade with basic phonemic awareness. Obviously, students come to kindergarten with different levels of these skills; instruction should be flexible enough to respond to differing needs. Most phonemic instructional activities start with extensive games and letter and word play and then move on to more formal activities such as blending oral sounds, identifying sounds, and representing sounds with letters.

These activities can still be game-like and thus should fit in well with other kindergarten activities.

A sophisticated range of phonemic awareness activities with spoken language has been developed during the past few years. These programs, now available for use in classrooms, have produced significant jumps in phonemic awareness.[5] They include rhyming activities; identifying the beginning, middle, or ending sounds or identifying words spoken in a broken fashion (/p/, /i/, /g/); identifying word families such as *s-ing, r-ing, th-ing;* counting or matching the sounds of words with counters and letters (Blachman, 1991, pp. 7-19; Griffith & Olson, 1992; Yopp, 1992); and training students to be aware of how their tongues and lips make sound (Lindamood & Lindamood, 1992).

Used in the classroom, phonemic awareness programs can have a tremendous impact on a child's learning. As an example, Blachman and Ball initiated a very successful phonological awareness training in inner-city kindergartens in upstate New York. Groups of four to five children were taught for 4 days a week for 11 weeks, for 15 to 20 minutes a day—the equivalent of approximately 11 to 15 hours of training. Kindergarten teachers and aides received 14 hours of in-service training (Blachman, 1991).

The lesson consisted of three parts. First, the children engaged in an activity called *say-it-and-move-it,* in which they represented each sound in a one-, two-, or three-phoneme word with a blank tile. Later, they used tiles with letters they had already learned to recognize. Research has shown that connecting letters and sounds is reciprocally related and enhances the teaching of both (Blachman, 1991, p. 11).

The second activity comprised a variety of segmentation-related activities, such as odd-picture-out. The third activity was learning letters and their sounds. Large increases in phoneme segmentation ability, letter knowledge, and reading and spelling occurred (Blachman, 1991, pp. 14-15). *Imagine the implications: Most children who will fail at beginning-reading tasks are only 15 hours away from removing a major barrier to succeeding in first grade, if the right intervention is provided early enough.*

The Lindamood-Bell Learning Process[6] also produces effective phonemic training, but the programs require more time with a broader representation of kindergartners. The strategies include some analytic word activities such as learning how sounds are made with the mouth and tongue; using chips to become conscious of words, sounds, similarities, and differences; then progressing to using letters; and finally, performing multisyllabic segment comparison tasks. More extensive phonemic awareness training may be necessary for extremely phonologically challenged children.

Whichever method is used, it is essential to ensure that every kindergarten child has the opportunity to receive the phonemic support he or she needs. This means a mid-kindergarten assessment of all youngsters on phonemic awareness scales that shows whether students know the segmental nature of speech. As an example, Yopp and Singer have devised a simple sound-segmentation task for kindergartners (Yopp, 1995). Children also need to be assessed periodically to determine progress with simple assessments, such as blending tasks; tasks identifying beginning, middle, and ending sounds in spoken words; and letter-to-sound mapping tasks. In addition, teachers need instruction on how to use more sophisticated assessments such as the Roper/Schneider test with subtests in phonemic segmentation, that is, What two sounds are in *no?*; blending; deletion of first phoneme; deletion of last phoneme; substitution of first phoneme; and substitution of last phoneme or the Lindamood-Bell LACT-R assessment (Juel, 1994, p. 7). The goal is effortlessness or fluency in these basic phonemic awareness tasks (Bowey, 1995, pp. 65, 67). Adams (1990, p. 331) also recommends phonemic training to recognize word families and the syllable patterns orally.

Print Awareness

Before they enter first grade, most middle-class youngsters have developed basic print awareness, or what Marie Clay (1991) calls "concepts about print," through more than 1,000 hours of parental attention that includes being read to and other print activities, such as playing with magnetic letters, puzzles, games, and so on. These concepts include the purpose of reading, the structure of written text, how stories work, what a word is, how words are composed of letters, what spaces signify, and directionality, that is, how print is organized, which necessitates the ability to scan left-to-right and then sweep diagonally left and one line down (Clay, 1991, pp. 141-154).

In contrast, many lower socioeconomic children have been read to for fewer than 50 hours and are way behind their middle-class peers in acquiring basic print awareness. These students must be given these experiences in Head Start programs, preschool programs, and kindergarten through a combination of language activities in which these concepts can be pointed out or through games that allow manipulation of letters, words, and sentences. Marie Clay (1991) has developed a widely used Concepts in Print assessment and has suggested a wealth of print awareness activities for children (pp. 145-154).

Mastering a Few Sight Words

In kindergarten, students should be able to recognize a few words (such as their own name) by sight.

Syntactic Awareness

Finally, teaching preschool and kindergarten students about sentences, phrases, and the order of words by bringing these concepts to their attention in reading activities or through manipulative games has been shown to improve reading ability (Clay, 1991, pp. 293-295). As Adams (1990) writes, "With respect to young readers, development of syntactic competence may be far more important than is generally recognized in reading instruction. Without the within-sentence phrasal and clausal boundaries that permit interpretive recoding, the young reader has no rational option but to try to conquer whole sentences at a time" (p. 415). Again, writing activities are another extremely effective method of developing these skills.

SUMMARY

Any successful reading program must start with a skills strand in preschool or Head Start and another in kindergarten. It must explicitly include activities that teach the names and shapes of letters and, as much as possible, their simplest sounds, since some have more than one. It must include beginning phonemic awareness and print and syntactic awareness, in addition to the strands that stress oral language; listening to, discussing, and retelling stories; and writing group stories.

Activities to develop oral language and print awareness have become widespread. Most preschools and kindergartens incorporate shared reading of stories with big books that enable a class of children to follow along. Robert Slavin's "Success for All" program, one of the most successful comprehensive reading programs (discussed in more detail in the next chapter), is research-based and has produced significant measurable results. It uses a strategy of having children retell stories to develop active engagement with books. Many teachers read and discuss good children's literature and write down dictated stories from the children or have children learn to write letters and try to write stories.

What is also needed is a *systematic* strategy for developing an increasing knowledge of the other important prerequisites for reading—knowing the names of letters, their shapes, and the more simple sounds associated with some of them, understanding the internal phonological structure of spoken words, and a basic understanding of syntax.[7]

Notes

1. Adams elaborates, "The orthographic processor cannot begin to learn spellings until it has learned to recognize the letters from which they must be built. The phonological processor cannot usefully learn letter sounds until the orthographic processor has learned to discriminate the individual letters with which they must be linked" (p. 362).

2. For a good summary of these ideas, see Hoorn, Nourot, and Scales (1993). According to these authors, children develop precursors to reading during ages 3 to 5 through play and investigations. These include

- Learning to use symbols to represent experiences (a block being used as a telephone)
- Taking the perspective of others
- Using increasingly efficient mental strategies to remember information and solve problems
- Predicting
- Developing story plays for self and their peers to "act out" and thus learning story grammars such as plot, character development, etc. (pp. 20-25, 133-147, 193-216, 220-225)

For two popular training programs based on Australian and New Zealand models and strong on whole-language techniques but weak on skills development see the Rigby associated ELIC (Early Literacy Inservice Course), Tel: (800) 822-8661, and "Frameworks," a K-8 literacy training program also based on the ideas of Marie Clay. Developed by Brian Cambourne, Jan Turbill, Andrea Butler, and Gail Langton, it is offered nationwide through the Office of Staff Development, Wayne-Finger Lakes, BOCES, 3501 Country Road 20, Stanley, New York 14561, Tel: (716) 526-4669.

3. English-speaking children in California could name on average 71% of uppercase letters by age 5. Spanish-speaking children could identify on average only 4%. See Adams (1990), p. 358, ft. 69. In contrast, most children learn to recite the letter names as in the Alphabet Song before age 4 or even age 3. For longitudinal studies on learning names well before shapes see Adams (1990), p. 360, ft. 77.

4. Blachman (1991) writes that "one of the fundamental tasks facing the beginning reader is to develop the realization that speech can be segmented and that these segmented units can be represented by printed forms. . . . As we now know from extensive research conducted during the last fifteen years, developing an awareness of the phonological segments in words is an important prerequisite to understanding how an alphabetic transcription represents speech. That transcription will make sense to beginning readers only if they understand that the transcription has the same number and sequence of units as the spoken word [citation omitted]" (pp. 5-7).

5. See study cited in Torgesen and Barker (in press) in which Wagner, Torgesen, and Rashotte looked at 13 phonological awareness training studies in 1993 and found large average effect size of about 1¼ standard deviations (moving a child from the 50th percentile to above the 70th) in phonemic awareness.

6. Lindamood-Bell Learning Process, 416 Higuera St., San Luis Obispo, California 93401, Tel: (805) 541-3836.

7. Some of the newest reading series offer a balanced approach between literature-based instruction and skills development that provides strands for phonics, word family study, phonemic, print, and syntactic awareness along with whole-language strategies. These materials offer letter recognition, phonemic awareness, concepts of print, syntactic understanding, and the other skills described in this section. Evidence for a balanced approach comes from some of our best teachers. For example, Laverne Apodaca, who was so successful in bringing inner-city children in San Francisco to the reading levels of students in the wealthiest areas of the state such as Beverly Hills or San Marino, is now working as a kindergarten teacher in an inner-city school in San Francisco with the aim of getting multilingual kindergartners starting to read by the end of the kindergarten year, as is routinely done in Spanish-speaking countries where the language is more phonically regular than English. (As an aside, one wonders why there are so many children in bilingual classes who can't read by the third grade, even in their primary language.) She is not using worksheets for these small children but direct instruction and activities which stress letter and sound acquisition and connection to appropriate text.

California State University at Long Beach professor Claude Goldenberg has conducted research in Los Angeles in which direct instruction in phonics (in Spanish) for Spanish-speaking kindergarten children produced significantly higher reading in first grade and beyond and was the most productive of all the methods he tried (much to Goldenberg's surprise) (Goldenberg, 1994, pp. 171-199).

4

Beginning-to-Read
Instruction for Early First Grade

Several issues are central to early first-grade reading instruction, as follows:

1. Students need to be taught enough about the phonemic, phonic, syntactic, and word structure systems and provided with sufficient word-attack and other self-teaching strategies to enable them to automatically recognize a critical mass of common words and know how to decode simple new words.

2. Once students attain this much control of the reading process, they can then begin to read larger and larger amounts of narrative and informational text. Reading more text of increasing complexity depends on two elements—becoming automatic with more words and increasing decoding skills. The reason automaticity is so important is that if students are to read for meaning, they can attempt to stop to figure out only about 1 word in 20; they must be automatically recognizing about 95% of the words. Since it takes between 4 and 15 successful attempts at an individual word before that word becomes automatically recognized (if decoded the first few times by looking

and hearing letter/sound correspondences), students need to read enough to become automatic with growing numbers of words. This increasing automaticity then increases the kinds of books they can read and still stay within the accepted range.

3. If instruction in the more complex decoding skills is also provided, even more material will be available to students. One of the main barriers to extensive reading is that in English, text is replete with many words important to the meaning of the passage but that occur infrequently (with little chance for the word to become automatic). Without a system for decoding these words independently, students are effectively cut off from much potentially engaging, instructionally important, but increasingly complex material.

4. Developing a growing pool of automatically recognized words and increasingly sophisticated decoding skills will enable students to read extensively and learn the rest of the phonics, syntax, and word structure systems as they tackle progressively more difficult books and stories. This independent and assigned reading should be monitored by teachers who provide reinforcement, guidance, continual assessment, and direct teaching to fill in the gaps.

In addition to quickening and broadening the processes of becoming fluent readers, extensive reading will also help students develop a love of literature, find out about the world through fiction and nonfiction, and enrich their lives. Simultaneously, instruction should include strands of reading to children, reading strategically, discussing material, writing, mechanics, and spelling.

If students are to reach this level—able to read and learn from trade books and basal texts without struggling with most words—then, as argued above, most of them will first need to be directly taught enough phonemic awareness, basic phonics, and word-attack skills in an organized, sequential, active-learning program. A key component of this strategy is guiding the student to think about the phonemic system (how sounds make up words), the graphophonic connections (which letter patterns make which sounds and words), the syntactic structures (do the words sound right in context?), and meaning (does the word make sense?) while students read high-quality stories and materials designed specifically to (or are appropriate to) reinforce the skills being taught. Also essential are writing and spelling activities that give students practice in translating sound and words into print.

The following sections discuss the essential details, strategy, and timing of each of the key skills that must be taught.

The Learning-to-Read Sequence

As delineated earlier, phonemic awareness is necessary for decoding, decoding is necessary for word recognition, and word recognition is the key to comprehension in first grade.

Connie Juel (1994) has written one of the clearest explanations of what it takes to teach low socioeconomic children to read and why in *Learning to Read and Write in One Elementary School.* She is another leading researcher who maintains that one of the clearest findings of research is that first-grade reading comprehension is almost exclusively determined by word recognition (p. 12). Lyon (1994) confirms these findings; the ability to read and comprehend depends upon rapid and automatic recognition and decoding of single words, and slow and inaccurate decoding are the best predictors of difficulties in reading comprehension (research cited, p. 11). Juel (1994) found that the ability to recognize single words in print accounted for 71% of ending first-grade reading comprehension among a group of poor children she studied (p. 17). The other major factor—listening comprehension or the ability to understand spoken words—only contributed 6%. Listening comprehension becomes much more important in second grade and beyond as material becomes more difficult and the ability to read words develops (Juel, 1994, p. 17).

Recognizing Single Words

Which key elements determine the recognition of single words? There are two: first, the ability to decode, or in Juel's words, "cipher knowledge"; and second, the memorized knowledge of the internal letter structure of particular words, or lexical knowledge. In first grade, decoding (cipher) knowledge is the key to word recognition, which in turn is the key to reading comprehension (Juel, 1994, p. 17).

Lexical knowledge is a combination of knowing enough cues about particular words and which rules apply for that word (e.g., knowing that the *o* in *come* is pronounced *uh* or *to* is pronounced like *you*). Lexical knowledge means these words are essentially memorized without knowing the more general letter/sound rules. Unfortunately, students who recognize a word this way cannot necessarily decipher new and different words. In first grade, lexical knowledge determines only about one fourth of the ability to recognize words, whereas ciphering or decoding determines about two thirds. By second grade, the contribution of ciphering goes down to one fourth and the automatic—unmediated by tracking letter to sound—lexical recognition jumps to more than one half of all words, as students become familiar with more and more words (Juel, 1994, p. 17). However, it is crucial that beginning readers establish the pathways for automatic retrieval of these rapidly recognized words through the tool of decoding which forces the mind to hear the word and allows for accessible storage and quick retrieval. As will be discussed later in this chapter, storing words in long-term memory without letter/sound patterns results in appreciably slower recognition.

Learning to Decode

Learning to decode (knowing letter/sound patterns and word-attack skills) in turn depends primarily on phonemic awareness (contributing about one half to decoding ability in both first and second grades), and secondarily on exposure to print (the number of words that have been read correctly). Exposure to print contributes about one third in first grade and one fourth in second grade to decoding ability (Juel, 1994).[1] Syntactic and context knowledge also help with decoding, but make much smaller contributions. Phonemic awareness is a prerequisite or corequisite for decoding skills. Attempting to teach phonics without attending to phonemic awareness is destined to fail (Juel, 1994, pp. 16-24). Lyon (1994) adds that "the ability to decode single words accurately and fluently is dependent upon the ability to segment words and syllables into abstract constituent sound units (phonemes). Deficits in phonological awareness reflect the core deficit in dyslexia [research cited]" (p. 11).

Juel (1994) reached her conclusions by following a cohort of low-income children from first to fourth grade. She determined which students were average or above in reading comprehension in the fourth grade and which were in the bottom quartile and then went back to the assessments made in early and late first grade, early and late second grade, and so on, to see which factors made the difference.

On a 42-item phonemic awareness scale, the students who ended up in the bottom quartile at the end of fourth grade scored about 4 at the beginning of first grade and only improved to 19 at the end of first grade. Members of the average-to-top group of readers started first grade at 21 (above where the low group finished) and went all the way to 38 (just about maximum on the phonemic awareness scale) by the end of first grade, a level not reached by the low group until the end of third grade. Thus, during the crucial period of early first grade when the average and good readers had the ability and desire to learn phonics, they did, and so learned to read. In contrast, the low group (remember, all these children came from similar backgrounds) learned very little about decoding—except bad habits and frustration. Because they were not taught phonemic awareness, they could not comprehend being asked to "say the first sound in apple," they could not learn to sound out a word, and they could not induce letter/sound correspondences from printed words.

As a result, on a ciphering test (which uses pseudowords such as *buf* and *dit* so memorized words make no difference), the average-to-good readers scored 25. The first 20 words on this test were simple consonant/vowel/consonant words, the next 20 were more complex such as *cleef*, and the last 10 were multisyllabic. The low group scored only 8 despite a year's instruction in phonics and reading (about 40% of the low group could not read one word on the list—all of these children had no phonemic awareness at the beginning of first grade). The good-reader group made substantial progress in second grade and hit very high levels on this phonics test by the end of third grade—in the 1940s—and then grew slightly after that. The poor readers progressed slowly from a lower base, hit 28 at the end of third grade and stayed there.[2]

Not remedying these students' lack of phonemic awareness early on, so that they can be taught the phonics systems early in the first grade, dooms almost all of these unfortunate children. Only one out of eight of these children will ever read on grade level (Juel, 1994, p. 24).[3] Reading becomes frustrating and embarrassing, with the result that these bottom quartile children begin to actively dislike reading and end up reading much less than their counterparts. Juel found that by fourth grade the average-to-top group read almost four times as much at home and twice as much in school. By fourth grade, only one out of five students in the poor reading group said unequivocally that they liked to read, in contrast to 9 out of 10 of the good-reader group.

Forty percent of the poor readers would rather clean their room than read compared to only 5% of the average- and good-reader groups. Or as one of the poor readers said, "I'd rather clean the mold around the bathtub than read" (Juel, 1994, p. 120).

By reading so little, these children cut themselves off from the best activity to improve their reading and thinking capacity in the primary years (Cunningham & Stanovich, 1993, p. 201; Stanovich, 1993). Low-income or second language children depend more heavily on school experiences to expand their vocabulary and conceptual knowledge than higher-socioeconomic-status children. For them and most other children, extensive reading is the major factor in producing further growth in listening comprehension, concept growth, and vocabulary growth, which in turn are all critical to further reading. Consequently, being able to read early becomes crucial in becoming more literate.

Reading and Comprehension

Juel's study of good- and poor-reading low-income children demonstrates how important widespread reading is in improving the conceptual capacity of low-income students. In that study, listening comprehension was extremely low for both groups in the beginning of first grade; both good and poor readers scored about 1.5 on a 6-point scale. By the end of second grade, the low group reached 2.5 on this listening test and did not improve after that. The average to top group improved to 3.2 at the end of second grade, to 4.9 at the end of third grade, and 5.2 at the end of fourth grade (Juel, 1994, p. 22).

Consequently, poor children can substantially improve their knowledge about the world, the depth of their conceptual understanding, and their vocabulary—all of which are key determinants of further advances in reading—by extensive in-school and home reading. In fourth grade, growth in listening comprehension slowed for the top group as the conceptual load of books in subjects such as science and history increased. At this stage further growth begins to depend more on instruction in strategic reading, effective comprehension such as deep discussions, experience in expository text and how to argue a point, word-root and syllabication skills, and more extensive reading, all of which are discussed in later chapters.

Thus the ability to read early becomes crucial to later reading success and those who miss out in the early first grade almost never recover. Stanovich (1986) called this phenomenon the "Matthew effect"—the rich get richer and the poor get poorer. Juel (1994) explains this phenomenon as follows:

> A lack of phonemic awareness severely limits children's growth in cipher knowledge, which in turn limits their ability to recognize words and to spell, which ultimately acts to constrain growth in listening comprehension and ideas that will in turn limit reading comprehension and writing. (p. 121)

In summary, without organized intervention during this critical early stage, the educational careers of these slow-to-start readers have already been determined. However, experts estimate that significant numbers of this bottom quartile can get on track by the end of first grade, either with effective initial teaching or rapid supplemental intervention when problems become apparent. Juel (1994), for example, enables three out of four students with extremely low levels of phonemic awareness in early first grade to achieve grade level in comprehension by the end of first grade. She reaches additional students during second grade through a tutoring program teaching phonemic awareness and deciphering mainly through reading, writing, and word activities aimed at learning these skills.

Practice Makes Perfect:
The Sequence of Becoming an Automatic Reader

Experience and research of the past two decades, including studies such as Juel's, have led educators Linnea Ehri (1994, pp. 325-343, in press) and David Share and Keith Stanovich (1995b, pp. 13-27; see also Share, 1995) to delineate the phases by which a student becomes an automatic reader. Share and Stanovich (1995b) call their model the "self-teaching model" *because the act of repetitive decoding of a particular word and connecting spelling to sounds (which they call "phonological recoding") helps establish the spelling patterns of that word in memory. Each time the letters in the word are read successfully, the sound is heard mentally, the pathways for access get stronger, and that word becomes a little easier to recognize the next time it is encountered, until reading it becomes automatic.* In the early stages of reading, it takes about four or five times of successfully decoding a word for it to become fully automatic. Encountering the word in the context of reading reduces the number of successful attempts necessary. (For some special education students, the number of necessary readings may reach 50 or 100.) The most effective way for students to become fluent with a specific word is for them to consciously process both the letter patterns and sounds of the word the first few times it is read (Ehri, 1994; Share, 1995; Share & Stanovich, 1995b). For beginning readers, a combination of repeated reading of familiar material and tackling new material builds a critical mass of automatically recognized words, which in turn multiplies the number of books a student can read (p. 45).

At the same time students are becoming automatic with a growing number of words, they are strengthening their ability to decode new words by establishing different patterns of spelling/sound correspondences. Finally, by repeated successful attempts at recognizing individual words, not only do those words become automatic, but the letter and sound pattern of each word also gets added to the generalized knowledge about the spelling sound system and is available to help decode other words.

Logographic, Alphabetic, and Orthographic Tools

Ehri (in press) postulates four overlapping phases in becoming automatic with a particular word (making the word a sight word): the pre-alphabetic or logographic; partial alphabetic; alphabetic; and consolidated alphabetic or orthographic. As children learn more about the alphabetic system, they incorporate this growing knowledge as additional and more powerful tools in learning to recognize words. These phases are not hard and fast, and as students are learning to become automatic with thousands of words, they use a mix of these strategies, with any particular child giving more emphasis to one tool or another. However, unless students become proficient with phonological recoding (decoding) and knowledgeable about the spelling structures required in the later phases, they will not become good readers. Context clues, or even being told a word when stumped, also help supplement the initial stages of learning to recognize a word and can speed up the process of retrieving a partially decoded word (Share & Stanovich, 1995b; Tunmer & Chapman, 1995), but as explained previously, these methods are too inefficient and too slow to be relied on as a major strategy for the self-teaching model.[4]

Pre-Alphabetic or Logographic Phase

The first phase, which is actually prereading, occurs early in kindergarten and is extremely short-lived. In this stage, children recognize words by distinct visual features or connected symbols such as the McDonald's arch, the patterns of letters in their name, or the two *os* in *moon*. This strategy does not take them too far because each word has different distinctions, most words' shapes are not that distinctive, and, most importantly, students have no method for reading new words. Too much reliance on shape and visual features can actually slow down the learning-to-read process (Share & Stanovich, 1995b, p. 20).

Partial Alphabetic Phase

The second phase, partial alphabetic, occurs after students acquire some early letter and sound knowledge, which for most children should be under way by the kindergarten years. Students look for partial correspondences between one or more letters such as the first or last letter in a word. This stage starts the path to rapid access to words through the alphabetic principal as students look for some letter/sound correspondence. Obviously, children need a basic level of phonemic awareness, knowledge of some specific letter shapes, and a smattering of specific letter/sound correspondences (Share & Stanovich, 1995b, p. 21). This partial decoding stage is helpful in starting to lay down in students' minds letter/sound correspondences in advance of learning functional decoding skills.

In addition, as Ehri's seminal 1994 work pointed out, this technique even works with learning irregularly spelled, high-frequency words in beginning texts (the consonants still follow a pattern; it is the vowels that are irregular) (Share & Stanovich, 1995b, p. 23). However, this strategy is not very effective in identifying words because many words are so similar in English (e.g., *house* and *horse*) and cannot be identified by partial decoding strategies.

Overlapping this partial alphabetic phase is the growing ability of beginning readers to recognize words by memorizing their spelling (logographical or lexical learning by the use of spelling patterns alone, as opposed to alphabetic learning), but without being able to sound out the word. This is the way many nonalphabetic languages, such as Chinese, are learned. Many kindergartners and first graders have memorized a considerable number of words, especially high-frequency words, without knowing decoding skills. But memorizing words as a strategy to learn to read has fatal flaws in English.

First, memorizing increasing numbers of words becomes a difficult burden for most children. According to Stanford University Education Professor Robert Calfee (1995, pp. 79-80), English calls for a deeper understanding of the alphabetic principle than other alphabetic languages because there are so many more basic three-letter consonant/vowel/consonant groups in English—more than 10,000 variations and far too many to learn by one-by-one memorizing. In Connie Juel's study, first-grade students (there were two groups) encountered 1,000 to 1,500 different words in their first-grade basal readers. In contrast, Chinese children who learn logographically—by the visual form of the word—learn only 3,500 characters in 6 years of school, and Chinese words and characters are much more visually distinctive (Juel, 1994, p. 11).

Second, memorizing words does not help children learn how to decipher the large number of new but infrequently encountered words that occur in English text. Thus, it is not a powerful enough technique to help them read increasing amounts of new material and capitalize on effective self-teaching strategies. These findings explain why, as previously discussed, lack of decoding ability is the primary reason students fail to progress in reading proficiency. This logographic as opposed to alphabetic strategy was the basis for the old "look-say method" that Chall (1983, 1989, 1992, 1995) found to be so much less effective than code-based strategies. Those students who did learn to read under look-say methods intuited the sound/symbol relationship. Many students never made the connection.[5]

Alphabetic Phase

In the next phase, called the alphabetic stage by Ehri (in press), students learn decoding, or how to match the simple one-to-one individual letter sound correspondences to the pronunciation of the word (phonological recoding). As more correspondences are learned, all the letters in a growing number of words can be decoded accurately; this will allow students to identify the right word and read much more material. In addition, by recoding the letters, effective mental access patterns are being established to help speed the process of automatic recognition. This alphabetic ability considerably extends the potential words that can be decoded and learned, increases the number of books that can be read, and allows more attention to meaning, as less time must be spent deciphering those words.

However, simple phonics, by itself, is not enough to achieve complete and automatic recognition for many irregular words that cannot be deciphered solely by attempting to match sounds to letters alone. For example, blending works for *sip* or even *slip,* but not for *slight.* Students must also be aided by the additional capacity of seeing larger chunks of letter patterns and some whole-word spelling patterns, translating those patterns into their pronunciations, and creating a representation of that pattern and word in memory—capabilities which also develop during this phase. Fortunately, these skills are more easily learned if a student knows how to recode. More importantly, letter/pattern sound recoding abilities help in decoding and remembering irregular words (Share & Stanovich, 1995b, p. 23). According to Share and Stanovich (1995b),

> Most irregular words, when encountered in natural text, have sufficient letter-sound regularity (primarily consonantal) to permit selection of the correct target among a set of candidate pronunciations. . . . [Thus], an approximate or partial decoding may be adequate for learning irregular words encountered in the course of everyday reading. (p. 23; see also Share, 1995, p. 166)

This alphabetic phase, usually occurring in early first grade, is when true reading can start. Students using this alphabetic strategy need to know decoding skills (mapping each letter and letter pattern to a sound), blending and word-attack skills, and a growing number of word-family spelling/sound patterns. Students also need to know how to apply these skills in reading for meaning and read enough text to expand their alphabetic knowledge. With repeated readings of particular words requiring enough decoding of that word's letters and hearing the sound of that word as a tool for creating a pathway to memory, the word gets easier and easier to read.

Two things then happen. One, recognizing that word becomes automatic and easy, which expands the number of words automatically recognized and thus frees mental energy for concentrating on meaning. Two, the spelling and sound patterns of that word become part of a growing generalized understanding of the spelling/sound system. Thus, as this stage progresses, patterns of regularity for both simple letter/sound correspondences and other more complex patterns develop.

Consolidated Alphabetic or Orthographic Phase

Gradually, the ability to recognize spelling/sound patterns develops both in terms of recognizing the higher frequency patterns and then, eventually, in terms of internalized rules (knowing the *ing* pattern, which neighboring letters make a *c* soft or hard, or patterns such as the *ough* in *tough* and *rough*). As students become familiar with the richness and breadth of spelling patterns, syllables, affixes, and word roots through extensive exposure to print and direct teaching, they can call on greater and greater assistance from these patterns to accelerate and ease decoding. This growing understanding of spelling patterns leads to the final phase, named the "consolidated alphabetic" or "orthographic" phase by Ehri (in press), which begins to appear in late first or second grade. As this phase progresses, students become automatic with most of the spelling patterns and their sounds.

In summary, every opportunity students have to successfully decode a variety of words advances the cause of their becoming automatic readers. The more sophisticated the tools beginning readers develop, the more text they can read and the more quickly they will become fluent readers.

Early First-Grade
Reading Components and Instruction

Based on knowledge of these sequences and how students learn to read, specific components have been delineated for inclusion in early first-grade skills instruction to develop students' ability to recognize words and learn new words from reading text. These components are as follows:

- Knowledge of all letter names and shapes and full print awareness
- More advanced phonemic awareness
- Understanding the system of basic letter and letter pattern/sound correspondences (phonics)
- Word-family instruction
- Decoding and word-attack strategies, for example, sounding out; recognizing comparable letter patterns from known words; learning to generate alternative pronunciations for ambiguous letter patterns (e.g., *bread*) and using context to resolve the ambiguity; recognizing word parts (e.g., *ing, ed*); self-correcting; and self-monitoring
- Beginning-writing and spelling activities as a strategy to learn reading
- Becoming automatic with high-frequency words and a growing number of other words
- Syntactic instruction, including the structure of sentences, clues from mechanics (such as punctuation and capitalization), and anticipation of words
- Vocabulary
- Improving listening comprehension
- Fluency (rereading and oral reading)

These skills should be taught explicitly and directly, not as rote learning, but in an active, problem-solving way. Students should be given ample opportunity to use these skills in reading for meaning with teachers, other adults, or partners.

Learning letter names and their shapes and print awareness was discussed in Chapter 3, "Beginning-to-Read Instruction for Preschool and Kindergarten." In early first grade, the other activities listed above should accompany continued instruction in listening to good stories and informational text and discussing their content, telling and retelling stories, listening to and singing nursery rhymes, giving explanations, and shared reading. These activities also should be dynamically related. For example, proficiency in letter/sound correspondences, phonemic awareness, word-attack and self-monitoring strategies, word families, and automatic recognition of high-frequency anchor words each works in tandem to contribute to deciphering text. The more proficient a reader is in each of these areas, the better the chances are that a word can be read.

Furthermore, the best instructional methods will use one skill to help learn the others. As one example, learning to recognize letter/sound correspondences enhances the latter stages of phonemic awareness; reciprocally, phonemic awareness exercises that use the letters to match sounds are highly effective methods of learning letter/sound correspondences. As another example, the activities of encoding spoken words involved in spelling and writing and the required attention to how print maps sounds are powerful tools in helping students learn the alphabetic principle.

Finally, all these skills should help students develop a conscious understanding of the spelling/sound system. Most top researchers and the best practitioners maintain that having active, thinking discussions with children—about connections, analogies, and comparisons of the details of the symbol/sound system and word-attack strategies as students tackle print—is one of the most successful teaching techniques for developing students' ability to use these tools while reading (Marilyn Adams, personal communication, April 1995; Cunningham, 1990).

In summary, the purpose of teaching each of these components is to give students a high-powered repertoire of tools—recognition and decoding strategies—that helps them become automatic with increasing numbers of words and continues to develop their decoding skills, thus enabling them to read more and more text and become fluent with more words. Depending on the requirements of the text, the extent of the student's background knowledge, and his or her decoding skills, a particular student will use the various skills at his or her disposal in various proportions to decode the word in the most efficient and speedy manner. Thus every student needs to be given the opportunity to learn the skills in each area and use these skills appropriately in decoding and reading for meaning so that he or she can learn to recognize a growing number of words automatically.

Joseph Torgesen (1995) writes that

The self-teaching model of reading acquisition has at least three clear implications for teaching reading to young children that are not typically followed. First, it suggests the importance of direct instruction to help at-risk children acquire some reasonable level of alphabetic reading skills very early in the reading instruction process. Furthermore, the model shows why early acquisition of these skills is so essential: they provide the tools by which the child's subsequent experiences

in reading text can contribute to the development of orthographic representations that are sufficiently specific to enable
accurate distinctions between words during fluent reading.
Second, the model suggests that there should be direct instruction to help children integrate the use of phonological clues
and context in order to arrive at accurate pronunciations of
words in text. Third, the model also shows why it may be very
important to provide training in phonological awareness,
either prior to or simultaneously with, early instruction in
phonics and text processing. (p. 92)

Based on these ideas, we know early first-grade skills instruction
should be organized around the following strands.

Completion of Letter
Recognition and Print Awareness

At the beginning of first grade, students need to quickly develop
full automatic recognition of every letter and complete print awareness. Most of these tasks should have been accomplished in kindergarten.

Phonemic Awareness Assessment and Instruction

First, students need to be assessed early for their phonemic
awareness level, and an organized support program should be provided for those who score below the levels necessary to profit by
phonics instruction. Dynamic strategies can then be used that incorporate learning phonemic awareness along with the other parts of the
sound/symbol system, especially the ability to blend sounds (Share,
1995). Second, the remainder of the students should increase their
phonemic awareness through learning the sound/symbol system with
the addition of some of the more advanced phonological manipulation
and syllable comparison tasks (i.e., exactly how two syllables differ in
phonemes) (Lindamood, Bell, & Lindamood, 1992). There is a strong
causal and reciprocal relationship between learning to decode and
developing phonemic awareness. Becoming proficient at one helps
proficiency in the other and vice versa (Blachman, 1991, p. 11;
Cunningham, 1990, p. 430; Share, 1995, p. 192).

One strong finding concerning the best method of teaching phonemic awareness—and actually any other skill—comes from a study by Anne Cunningham (1990) who contrasted ways of teaching two groups of first graders phonemic segmentation and blending tasks. One group just learned the tasks. The other split the time between learning the tasks and discussing and practicing how best to apply these skills. This second group was helped to reflect on and discuss the value, application, and utility of phonemic awareness—the students talked about how to use it in reading. Although both groups improved significantly in phonemic awareness compared to a control group, the group that received the conceptual or metacognitional level of instruction improved significantly more in reading comprehension (the skill-and-drill group improved to the 52nd percentile while the metacognitional group improved to the 70th percentile) (Cunningham, 1990, pp. 439, 441-442). Metacognition and conscious use should be built into any phonemic training strategy.

Benita Blachman (1991, pp. 16-18), who conducted the kindergarten phonemic awareness program discussed earlier in Chapter 3, also developed a five-step first-grade program that illustrates how phonemic awareness training can support a beginning-reading program for children at risk of failure. The children in this program were some of those who had received the kindergarten program described earlier.

First, teachers reviewed the sound/symbol associations for a few minutes and introduced a new sound. Then they emphasized phonemic analysis using a Slingerland technique (named after one of the pioneers in teaching dyslexic children), in which a small pocket chart of letters, color coded for vowels and consonants, allows students to represent each phoneme in a word with its corresponding letter as the teacher pronounces it. After that, students would change the word to another word such as *sat* to *sit* and engage in other word-building activities. In the next segment, these words were put on cards to be practiced for automatic recognition. High-frequency sight words were also introduced. This segment took a brief 2 to 3 minutes. The next segment was story reading, in which students tried to consciously apply the learned skills; this occupied most of the time. The program used phonetically controlled readers, stories from basal readers, and trade books. Finally, there was a written dictation exercise of the words that had been produced earlier on the sound board and from the reading. Significant gains were produced compared to similar children who did not receive this program.

Letter and Letter Pattern/Sound Correspondences Instruction

All students need a structured program in order to learn enough of the letter and letter pattern/sound correspondences so that they can recognize an adequate number of words to start reading, learn to decode new words, understand the alphabetic principle that words are made up of letter/sound correspondences, and extend their phonemic awareness as described earlier. They must also learn how the letter/sound system works, so that they can learn many of the remaining correspondences by themselves with minimal teacher support. Most students who possess little literacy preparation or who have auditory, visual, or memory problems need to continue a structured program for an extended period of time to learn the bulk of these correspondences. Other students will be able to learn the remaining correspondences fairly quickly through a more flexible program.

Learning the letter/speech sound connections of the English language is much trickier than is commonly appreciated for several major reasons. As Adams (1990) emphasizes, it is not just a case of teaching the letters and their corresponding sounds. In the chapter titled "On Teaching Phonics First" (pp. 237-292) of her 1990 book, *Beginning to Read: Thinking and Learning About Print,* Adams covers thoroughly the information in this and the following paragraphs about learning spelling/sound correspondences.

First, in English there is not a simple one-to-one correspondence between each letter and each sound. Some letters—for example, all of the vowels and some of the consonants—can map to several potential sounds, such as *c* to *city* or *county*. Sometimes a combination of letters maps to a unique sound such as the *ch* in *chair.* There are approximately 50 letter or letter combinations (called graphonemes) that can represent a phoneme in a word. Conversely, there are about 40 different phonemes in spoken English, many of which are represented by single letters or multiple-letter combinations such as the /f/ sound, which can be represented by the letters *f, ff,* or *ph.*

Because of these multiple representations, there are hundreds of correspondence pairs in English, all of which eventually must be learned until they are securely lodged in memory and available for searching when a reader is trying to match the spelling patterns of the word being deciphered to the sounds of the word. Even when restricting the word universe to one- and two-syllable words found in reading materials of 6- to 9-year-olds, researchers found 211 spelling/sound correspondences. Not all of these must be learned by the end of first grade, and many can be learned by the maturing reader without being taught by knowing how the sound system works and reading large amounts of text.

But, at the start, some of the common correspondences have to be directly taught, blended, used in reading, and checked. Older phonics programs moved very slowly through a structured approach to teach correspondences through the first and second grades. Adams (1990) found that these reading programs taught 170 correspondences by the second grade at a rate of an average of 2 per week. The more effective, newer programs, some of which are described later in this chapter, are more accelerated for some children, use a greater variety of materials such as trade books and multilevel reading materials written and adjusted for different rates of learning, and place heavier emphasis on independent reading.

Word Play and Word Work

Building words is one of the most effective strategies for learning letter/sound correspondences. For example, Robert Calfee has designed a program named *Metaphonics* (Moran & Calfee, 1993). This program provides a daily 10- to 20-minute word playtime during which 8 to 12 students construct words. Children first learn three consonants and a vowel, use the letters to make and pronounce words, and then rapidly add several more consonants and vowels. The lessons aim at having the children produce words, discuss among themselves how best to do this, and thus help them achieve conceptual understanding. This strategy treats students as fellow investigators (or in Calfee's words, "budding cryptographers") and problem solvers, while integrating decoding and spelling.

What Sequence?

As reasoned above, one of the major reasons to teach symbol/sound correspondences is to help students understand the idea that letters and letter combinations map to the sound segments of speech. Most will not understand this principle simply by being told it is true or even by being shown one or two examples. Many students will get the point only if they see example after example of this idea and are asked to think about the connections. Thus it is important to first introduce students to those correspondences that are the cleanest and easiest to perceive, such as consonants and the short vowels, and wait until later to teach potentially confusing alternative mappings. For example, although the sound of a long vowel is more obvious, whether it takes that sound is complicated by which letter or letters follow the vowel. That is why most code-emphasis or phonics-based strategies first teach the consonants, which can be demonstrated as the first or last sound of the word, and the short vowels.

Second, the initial pairs that are taught should include the clearest examples of sounds. It is easy to get a clear picture of an individual letter; sound segments are much more elusive and overlap with other sounds in speech. Thus, among the consonants, it is easiest to produce the phonemes for the letters *f, m,* and *s* that make an *fff, mmm,* and *sss* sound, respectively—sounds that are very close to the actual phoneme. Use of these correspondences such as in blending the sounds of *s,* short *a,* and *m* and understanding that the combination represents the word *sam* eliminates distractions. In contrast, try to say the phoneme for the letter *b:* It is impossible. You either say *bee* or *buh,* both of which contain two sounds, which is why many children get confused when trying to blend the sounds of *bat.* They must learn to disregard as only an approximation the extra sounds in *buh* and *tee* to get *bat.* Teachers should use the techniques developed to help avoid confusion when students learn to blend.

Finally, there is the problem of letters such as vowels that can represent multiple sounds. Think of all the different sounds *a* can stand for—*at, ate, far, data,* and so on. Adams (1990) recommends spacing the teaching of the alternative spelling/sound correspondences for a given letter over a period of time, when feasible. This way the student learns the first correspondence well before the second is introduced, but it is not so set in memory that it fights against laying down the second alternative in memory.

There is a variety of recognized sequences of phonics that progress from the easier consonants and vowels, singly or in combination, to the more difficult ones. The different approaches possess some common attributes. All programs include the basic 35 correspondences—the 21 consonants (including *y*); the "short" pronunciations of the five primary vowels that most three-letter words follow (e.g., *hot, sit, sat, can,* and *gun*); two from the long vowels as in *made* and *nice;* r- and l-controlled vowels as in *ball* or *for;* the initial consonant clusters *sl* or *br;* the initial consonant digraphs *sh* and *ch;* and the final consonant digraph *ck.* Obviously, learning these 35 correspondences does not enable a child to read anything of much interest. The remaining letter combinations are spread among those categories and four others: double consonants, final consonant clusters, vowel variants, and an "other" category including the *y* in *cry* and *penny,* the *igh* in *night,* the final syllable *el* and *le,* and the suffixes *sion* and *tion.*

Most effective programs teach enough of each of these 10 categories that children can learn the rest by themselves. How much is enough will depend on the child. Of course, the teacher must monitor the child's reading and fill in knowledge gaps in these correspondences after the child has completed this introductory stage. Many children need assistance well into the second grade; some learning disabled children need help for even longer. One can see the dilemmas teachers face in deciding how best to proceed, but any successful school must figure out a method and adopt materials that systematically ensure that each student eventually will become fluent with each of these correspondences.

How Much Practice?

For many children, both letters and letter combinations and their phonological correspondences are not easy to remember because they are confusing, abstract, and meaningless. In order to achieve a level of automatic recall and understand the system well enough to apply it to new words, they must invest a significant amount of time practicing recalling these combinations in a variety of reading circumstances.

For students who enter the classroom with a tremendous amount of prior experience with print, the initial symbol/sound lessons will be more review and clarification than introduction of new materials, that is, most will already know the sounds of consonants. The teacher can proceed fairly quickly to help those students perceive and become automatic in the overall system of the connections of letter patterns to sound. Because of their experiences with print, these students will also understand why the lessons are being taught and most will be highly motivated.

Students who have not had the background or who have visual, auditory, or memory processing problems must spend much more time on these lessons, including the reading of connected text with the teacher or receiving specially tailored instruction. This reality necessitates some differentiation of instruction or supplemental support from tutors or the teacher and aides. This is discussed later in this chapter.

If enough class time is devoted to learning these key letter/sound correspondences and other essential code-breaking skills and learning or reinforcing those skills in the context of reading appropriate stories, and if these are followed by a significant amount of reading and teacher and classmate discussion, most students should learn almost all the pairs thoroughly by the end of second grade, although some will not achieve this level until the third grade. Initially, the vehicle for instruction and follow-through should be materials designed specifically for or appropriate to these lessons. When students are capable of reading both narrative and informational trade books, magazines, and stories in textbooks, those materials should become the major—but not the only—vehicles to learn the remainder of these letter/sound correspondences, as well as to develop the ability to extend comprehension, discuss the stories or articles, and increase the number of books read.

A Major Caution About Letter/Sound Correspondences

If the English language mapped letter to sound as regularly as the Spanish language and had the regular and short consonant and vowel syllabication of Spanish, then some of the potential confusions among students and the teaching profession would be avoided. One of the problems in teaching a whole set of possible sounds for a given letter or letter combination is that in learning this complicated array, both teachers and students often forget the purpose of the exercise. Its purpose is not just to generate alternative sounds for a given letter or letter combinations; it is also to assist students' mental retrieval systems by etching in memory more and more symbol/sound relationships. Then later, when looking at the letter patterns in a particular word, the reader can effectively search for the appropriate sounds that decipher that word and unlock its meaning, so that the meaning of the word can be used in understanding the passage being read.

Furthermore, understanding simple letter/sound correspondences, although critical for becoming a proficient reader, is only one of the several mental processes necessary for automatic recognition of words. First, many words do not follow a one-to-one match of letters to sound and must be decoded by recognition of more complicated spelling pattern and sound relationships or by generating alternative pronunciations until one fits. Second, as explained previously, knowing letter/sound links is only one component of a series of complicated and dynamic mental processes triggered by attending to a pattern of letters. These processes interact simultaneously to conduct a search for the word stored in memory that matches potential combinations of the particular visual letter patterns in the word being read and the potential sounds associated with those patterns stored in memory. These processes search for likely word candidates and screen out unlikely ones, determine if any of the dwindling list of possible word candidates makes sense in light of what already has been read and the structure of the phrases and sentences of the passage, and, finally, make conscious the exact word that meets all the requirements.

The effectiveness and speed of this search depends on how well letters and letter patterns and the structure of the phoneme system have been incorporated in long-term memory, how practiced the reader is in using these systems in parallel, and how effectively the reader can use the meaning of what has been read so far to determine whether potential words would be appropriate. Relying on phonics instruction alone to carry the burden of developing facility in all these areas will not work. Instruction and practice must develop the dynamics of the total system.

Word Families

Students should learn to recognize automatically a growing number of key letter patterns or sequences that make up components of many words. An example of a common sequence is the word family (Adams, 1990, p. 321; Foorman, in press). A word family, or phonogram, consists of words with an easily recognizable pattern based on the same sounds, such as the *ent* in *went, sent, tent,* or *spent* or the *at* in *bat, sat, cat, flat,* or *splat.* These similar phonological structures, which are between syllables and phonemes, are called *rimes.*

According to Adams (1990, p. 321), the development of the ability to recognize a rime and its beginning consonant or blends, called the *onset,* should be a key strategy in learning to read. Word families are phonetically regular except for a few cases and could comprise a substantial part of beginning-reading text. As many as 500 words can be derived from just 37 rimes, most of which should be recognized by mid-first grade. (Another approximately 200 regular rimes should be recognized by the end of first grade.) Automatic recognition of key letter patterns significantly speeds up the process of seeing letters, translating them into sounds, and retrieving from memory the word and its meaning that correspond to that pattern. However, beginning-reading stories and materials must be designed specifically to highlight and reinforce these word-family relationships and organized so books are available to provide reading material for any particular word family being taught. Most current beginning-reading materials are not designed with these ideas in mind; only a few of the recently published materials incorporate this strategy.[6]

Decoding or Word-Attack Strategies

Preliminarily, the ability to decode has two poles. The first is the ability to recognize a word instantly and effortlessly by a quick visual scan of its letter patterns (aided by context and syntax). Instructional strategies that provide students with myriad opportunities to read individual words successfully numerous times will develop automatic recognition of an increasing number of words. The second pole is the more deliberate, conscious figuring out of a word not immediately recognized, by applying knowledge of the mapping system (Beck & Juel, 1995, p. 22). Word-attack proficiency is critical for two major reasons. First, the most effective way to become automatic with a particular word is to consciously process both the letter patterns and sounds the first few times it is read. Second, because so many words important to meaning appear infrequently and because most reading materials will contain substantial numbers of new words, student need an effective system of decoding new words in order to have access to most materials.

If students are to become independent readers of beginning materials by mid-first grade, learn to be self-teachers, and extend their reading abilities, they must have conscious command of several word-attack strategies to decode unfamiliar written words. These strategies include sounding out, comparing to known words or letter/sound patterns, generating alternative pronunciations and using content to choose the right one, recognizing word parts, using cueing system clues, self-monitoring, and self-correcting.

Sounding out consists of looking at the letters or patterns of letters, knowing or approximating the sounds those letters represent, and blending together those sounds to make what they recognize as a word that corresponds to a word they can already recognize and understand in speech, referred to as their speaking/listening vocabulary. This method is the most efficient mechanism to learn how to process new or not fully learned letter/sound combinations. An important point is that sounding out or any other word-attack strategy does not have to generate the exact word but only get close enough so that the mind makes the right connection, much like placing a paper clip closer and closer to a magnet until it is caught. Sounding out a word also forces students to look at and attend to the spelling pattern in the word, a crucial step in laying down the retrieval patterns in their long-term memory, which will eventually result in automatic recognition of that word after several successful decodings. Thus, every successful incidence of sounding out a word reinforces visual identification and is one more step in achieving automaticity with that word.

As discussed earlier, many children who have had experience with print have memorized a significant number of words visually (without phonological recording), and through reading beginning material, they will memorize more. However, they cannot learn enough words in this manner to read the bulk of material they will eventually encounter, and retrieving the word from memory will also be slower than if they had phonologically recorded it.

Even in first- and second-grade materials, more than a third of the words occur only once; the majority occur five times or fewer. With so few learning opportunities, learning words one word at a time will not provide adequate growth in the students' visual vocabulary. Students must develop the ability to decipher unfamiliar written words through reading a large amount of material with those patterns, and practicing with other reinforcement exercises. These activities will accelerate the recognition of those specific words and other words with related spelling/sound patterns. As a point of interest, most words read in first and second grade are already stored in memory as part of students' spoken language. Later on, readers confront the additional problem of deciphering a written word they do not know the meaning of, intuiting or learning that meaning, and installing that newly learned word in memory.

Very quickly, students encounter a major stumbling block in learning to read—many letter patterns in unknown words can have more than one pronunciation, and simple sounding-out strategies will not automatically generate the right candidate (*bread* can be pronounced like *red* or *reed;* or, more challenging, *react,* when first seen, could be pronounced *reeked, wrecked,* or *re-act*). Students must learn to generate legitimate pronunciation alternatives and use context clues to resolve the differences. David Share (1995) maintains that this difficulty is the "quintessential problem of reading acquisition" and that "independent generation of target pronunciations for novel orthographic patterns" is a critical skill in learning to read (p. 200).

In addition, through guided reading with the teacher or with partners, students should start to learn other strategic skills, such as thinking if they already know the word being deciphered or if it is similar to one they already have decoded; knowing how to break words apart by syllables or word endings such as *ing;* looking for little words within bigger words; reading in phrases; rereading; self-monitoring ("Can *duck* can be the right guess for *bird* if the first letter of the written word has a /*b*/ sound and *duck* starts with a /*d*/ sound?); use of other graphophonic, semantic, and syntactic clues; and self-monitoring and self-correcting (Clay, 1991, pp. 237-345).

Pressley and Cariglia-Bull (1995, pp. 42-45) discuss several of these techniques, including a decoding by analogy strategy that uses 120 key words to exemplify the vowel sounds.

Writing and Spelling as Strategies to Learn Reading

Another strategy essential to helping students learn phonic and phonemic awareness is to provide *daily* practice encoding the letter/sound correspondences being taught. This includes assigned writing activities or writing as part of the guided reading sessions with children (Foorman, in press) and writing the words being read for examples of the phonics principles being taught.

Temporary or approximated spelling techniques (in which children approximate the spelling of the words they hear or want to write) are also very useful, especially in giving teachers constant information about how well a student is learning particular letter/sound correspondences or phonemic awareness (see further comments on invented spelling in Chapter 6). Subsequent activities based on that diagnosis can be used to improve learning and give students additional practice in connecting sounds to letters.

Students should also be learning to write stories, descriptions, persuasions, and reports, and they should be receiving beginning instruction in mechanics (such as punctuation and capitalization) and grammar and usage.

High-Frequency Words

The fifth major task preliminary to reaching the trade book or preprimer level is to start to develop automatic recognition of an increasing number of the most frequently used words, such as *the, of, to, you,* and *was.* These words, which comprise a large number of the words of running text, are mostly phonetically irregular (they cannot be sounded out). Fortunately, although the vowels are irregular, many of the spelling/sound correspondences of the consonants are regular and help establish the spelling and phonetic pattern to facilitate memorization. Of the 150 most frequent words in printed school English, only 35 are "soundable" in the sense that both vowels and consonants are regular (Adams, 1990, p. 274). Estimates are that students should learn to recognize a pool of 50 of these words by December or January of first grade.

Syntactic Awareness

Students should be provided with further instruction in the structure of sentences, using clues from mechanics, such as capitalization and punctuation, and anticipation of words.

Listening Comprehension and Vocabulary

During the important early first-grade period, it is essential for students to also hear good stories with new concepts, new ideas about the world, and new vocabulary. They need to participate in deep and extensive discussions about those stories to prepare them for the texts they will read. Even though development of listening comprehension is not essential to the first stages of reading—which depends on recognizing printed words already in the child's spoken vocabulary—listening comprehension becomes much more important in the second grade, and because growth of vocabulary and concepts takes time, these activities should not be slighted. Many students also need to develop a "sense of story" for their writing activities. This stems from exposure to engaging stories.

Fluency

Some time should be devoted to accelerating reading speed by concentrating on phrasing, oral reading with proper inflection, and other such techniques.

Rereading

One of the best strategies for developing fluency in reading is rereading material until it becomes automatic. Rereading helps in two situations. In the first, students need to slow down in a passage to sound out or figure out a word. In concentrating on this task, they normally forget the most recently read string of words kept in their short-term memory to support deciphering words. Once they comprehend the difficult word, they need to go back to the start of the phrase or sentence to put the previous string of words and their meaning back in their short-term memory. Rereading a sentence or passage to clarify or reinforce what has been read is another example of this first situation.

In the second situation, students are introduced to a new book and they read fairly slowly as they are guided through it. They should read the book several more times until reading it is automatic. Then, the book should go into a class library where the student will have the opportunity to read the book several more times. This overlearning of words helps promote automatic reading (for example, Johnson and Louis [1990] support the importance of rereading and stress the usefulness of familiar nursery rhymes that students read over and over). There must be a large number of books in the classroom to support this strategy. Faster students may become bored with rereading and should be allowed to read new material if they wish to.

Note that the rereading discussed in this section is different from the questionable strategy of holding children back when they fail to satisfactorily complete a reading primer because of lack of decoding or phonemic knowledge. These students are assigned to read the same book in a new group, but without effective intervention to help them with phonemic awareness and decoding, they may learn to read the words in that book, but still not be able to tackle new words (Juel, 1994, p. 129). Rereading, on the other hand, involves students' choosing books to read again to become more fluent with that material as a supplement to their lessons and guided reading.

Individual Diagnosis and Benchmarks: Keys to Effective Instruction

As discussed in the kindergarten section, instruction must be sensitive to the stages of literacy development and individual needs and thus must be diagnostically driven. Initially, that means assessing each student in the areas of phonemic awareness, reading comprehension, listening comprehension, word recognition, decoding, lexical or spelling knowledge, and concepts in print (Juel, 1994, p. 121).[7]

One effective organizational strategy is to observe children's efforts in these areas, assess their progress, and monitor each of them closely in order to gauge who is not progressing quickly enough. A teacher can then tailor programs from that knowledge. For example, if a student does not possess enough phonemic awareness to profit by phonics, he or she needs an organized intervention program and additional word and sound play and activities. A student who is not making progress on the Bryant ciphering test (using pseudowords) or a comparable test also needs special help. Alternatively, as discussed below, a teacher needs to keep a running observational record of how each child is reading or spelling, which mistakes he or she makes, and which self-correction strategies he or she uses. Instruction should reflect the differing and changing needs demonstrated by these ongoing assessments.

Practicing Skills While Reading for Meaning
With a Teacher, Adult, or Student Partner

One of the major dilemmas of the first-grade teacher is how to quickly and adequately prepare children to read trade books or stories in basal texts. As discussed earlier, after a short period of time, the strategy of just teaching letter/sound correspondences or memorizing sight words in isolation without trying to apply that skill in an actual reading situation becomes ineffective with many children. Many students get bored; they don't see the point of the exercises, and they stop trying.

More importantly, combining reading materials that reinforce and elaborate what has been taught in introductory lessons (connected reading) with discussions about how the sound/symbol and language structure systems work in the specific material read is one of the most powerful strategies for learning and reinforcing those skills and being able to apply those skills in the meaningful task of reading (Adams, 1990, p. 234; Juel, 1994, pp. 129-130). (Another essential strategy, writing and spelling lessons designed to reinforce skill lessons, was discussed earlier in this chapter.)

Furthermore, receiving on-the-spot feedback from the teacher, other adult, or student partner who assists the student in learning how to apply the skills and seeing the obvious link between learning phonics and reading text also enhances the effectiveness of phonics instruction. Connected reading provides the meaningful exercise necessary for linking spelling patterns with the rest of the cognitive system, whereas phonics without connected reading amounts to useless mechanics and is too easily forgotten. Students also must practice integrating all the skills being learned in the actual act of reading for meaning—or, as in Michael Pressley's analogy, children who are learning to play baseball need to practice hitting and catching, but they also must learn to use these skills in an actual game (Pressley & Rankin, 1994, p. 166). Most importantly, reading should be fun. The earlier in their education that students can read a variety of high-quality books and materials by themselves or with a teacher, the more they will want to read.

On the other hand, reading for meaning cannot take place if the students are struggling over every word. A student who wishes to read a beginning book must have an already-developed critical mass of automatically recognized words and sufficiently honed decoding skills. Too many new words in a passage and underdeveloped decoding skills lead to frustration and discouragement. Furthermore, when too many words are unknown, students don't have enough mental energy left over after deciphering to attend to meaning. Students should use initial texts that provide them with high success rates in deciphering words. Clay (1991, p. 297) and Juel (1994, p. 122) state that for instructional purposes, students should be able to read at least 90% of the words, and for independent reading, they should be able to read approximately 95% of the words. Students need to be reading just at the level of being stretched, so that they get enough practice in how the sound/letter system works, learning new words, and becoming more proficient in using cueing systems to read for meaning without becoming so frustrated that they lose focus.

Specifically Designed Books and Materials

Researchers have found that the existence of the right number and kind of decodable words in beginning-reading texts is one of the most important factors in developing children's word recognition. They also found that phonics lessons made little sense to children beginning to read if few of the words in their initial texts did not follow these regular letter/sound correspondences (Adams, 1990, pp. 276, 279-280).

However, teachers frequently encounter difficulty in finding books and materials that will reinforce the initial phonics lessons. One solution is for book publishers to design more small books, stories, or reading activities that are appropriate to the skills being taught. These books or materials need to be intrinsically engaging, and while they may include some more complicated words, they must also include words that correspond to the phonics and word-attack lessons taught; have a number of potentially decodable words and word families that are clustered, repeated, and presented in such a way to emphasize their decodability; and present the sight words being taught or already taught. Students should read these books primarily for the stories and meaning.

These specifically designed or appropriate books should not constitute all the books or materials students read and discuss or that are being read to them. There are also other criteria for selecting texts, such as the complexity of the language structure. Connected text materials are merely a portion of the total reading program.

An instructional strategy to avoid is one that provides for whole-class phonics lessons (especially when many students do not have the phonemic awareness to benefit from them) that are detached from reading and do not give students the opportunity to apply those decoding lessons in reading text. Juel (1994) looked at a group of students who, while still in readiness workbooks, were given whole-class phonics for 20 to 30 minutes a day. By November, the lessons had covered all 26 letters as well as 14 digraphs and blends—enough to read all 20 pseudowords on the Bryant decoding test. Children did not get to practice the lesson in tailored materials and no check was made of phonemic readiness. This strategy proved highly ineffective. The proportion of students who could pronounce a particular consonant in either initial or final position ranged from .37 to .67. Only about half the children learned each consonant. More damaging, the average score for correct sounding out of the 20 words was 6, with most children scoring 0 correct (Juel, 1994, p. 125). Isolated phonics instruction did not teach these students to internalize the letter/sound system.

Another misguided instructional strategy cited by Juel (1994) is the use of worksheets or workbooks with some groups of children while other children work with the teacher. First, these activities are also isolated from practice in actual text reading. Second, workbook assignments are usually not individualized; they are assigned whether the child knows the skill or not. Juel found few children needed help on letter recognition, yet they spent one third of their time doing worksheets on that relatively useless activity. Some children needed no help in any of the letter recognition, sight word recognition, and phonemic discrimination tasks. Yet they were still doing worksheets instead of reading for a purpose, as in class projects, participating in book clubs, or simply reading. Third, circling letters on a sheet does not help develop letter/sound correspondences or phonemic awareness because such work lacks an oral component. Children who can circle a beginning sound already have the skill (Juel, 1994, pp. 128-129). Although some tailored worksheet activities can be effective, uncritical, unguided use of worksheets to teach the complicated letter/sound and phonemic systems probably does more to discredit a skills approach than any other factor.

Correctness Versus Coverage

An important corollary of pitching the material just right is the necessity of pacing a student's reading to allow him or her to read every word correctly. One of Juel's most important findings was that students (all from low-income circumstances) who read the core basal text with 95% accuracy scored significantly above average on reading comprehension scores at the end of first grade, whereas all children who recognized less than 60% of the words of their basal text scored below the 38th percentile in reading comprehension (Juel, 1994, pp. 122-124). Amazingly, this relationship held regardless of the number of words read. Whether students read as few as 4,000 words in running text or as many as 31,000, the ability to identify individual words that had been read was more important than how many stories were read.

Juel (1994) explains that cipher knowledge determines first-grade comprehension, and if the child develops good cipher knowledge, it does not matter how many words are read. (This finding only applies to first grade. In later grades, the amount of text read becomes important, although correctness still matters. Thus, by second grade, both correctness and coverage count equally. As stated before, reading text helps lexical knowledge, which becomes more important in contributing to word recognition; listening comprehension becomes more important to reading comprehension; and extensive reading is the best way to develop those skills.)

Juel (1994) writes that

> Most children do not appear to gain cipher knowledge merely by seeing lots of words. First-grade teachers must make sure that children learn to read the words in their readers. Sheer

coverage of stories will not compensate for, nor remediate, poor decoding skills. Quality of word recognition in first grade (i.e., being able to recognize words) is more important than quantity of exposure to words. On the other hand, once there is high quality word recognition, then and only then does quantity of reading become critical. (p. 124)

The Importance of
Timely, Early Intervention

During the last decade, schools have paid increasing attention to programs that provide rapid and early intervention or tutoring strategies for those students who are already slipping in the first grade because they are so deficient in skills. A successful reading program must have a strand that deals with this problem. The same strategies also can be applied after the first grade, but the payoff is highest if students are put back on track quickly.

Juel's 1994 study examined the progress during first grade of two groups of low-income students: those who scored average or above in reading comprehension at the end of first grade and those who scored poorly in comprehension at the end of first grade. On the 20-item first-grade Bryant test of ciphering knowledge (reading pseudowords), the first group scored 7 in October, 13 in December, and 18 in February. In contrast, the scores of the poor reading group were below 1 in October, 3 in December, and 6 in February, but most poor readers scored 0. These students obviously did not learn how the system of letter/sound correspondences works after a half year of detached phonics lessons isolated from basal instruction. Their writing showed similar deficiencies and many were selective-cue readers who recognized words only if they recalled enough of their letters. Some poor readers were just getting the idea of the alphabetic principle at the end of first grade when school closed (Juel, 1994, pp. 125-126). Some form of tutoring seemed essential for these students before midyear of first grade and most of them needed to have had intervention or assistance in phonemic awareness in kindergarten.

"Reading Recovery," which is discussed later in this chapter, is a 30-minute-a-day individual tutoring strategy that successfully helps students at the very bottom of the reading spectrum. It is a relatively expensive program because a highly trained professional reading specialist sees only one student at a time for a period of 8 to 12 weeks.

Consequently, only a small portion of a first-grade class can be assisted by one "Reading Recovery" teacher. Because of these issues, questions have been raised as to whether it is wise to rely on "Reading Recovery" as the major strategy in solving a school or district's reading problems.[8] The best approach is to treat "Reading Recovery" and other comparable tutoring or rapid intervention programs as a necessary component of a larger, more comprehensive reading improvement strategy.

Individual and Group Tutoring

"Reading Recovery" is only one of many options for schools needing rapid intervention for their students. Other programs have achieved similar results with programs such as Bob Slavin's "Success for All" which utilizes afternoon one-to-one tutoring, in combination with the several other reading improvement components described above, for the bottom tier of students.

Other researchers have developed successful strategies that use nonprofessional tutors or small group tutoring strategies. In *Getting Reading Right From the Start,* Elfrieda Hiebert and Barbara Taylor (1994) explain these approaches. Both Hiebert and Taylor have projects that utilize 20-minute tutoring of a group of the lowest students by the classroom teacher or an aide in the afternoon. These projects specifically teach word-attack skills and phonemic awareness, require writing and reading small books, and continually monitor students for progress. Connie Juel trains college students and other community volunteers to tutor in reading skills. A project professional monitors the daily lessons they teach. For about $600 per child, her tutoring projects in Texas and Virginia can get three out of four lagging first graders on track by the end of first grade after approximately 40 sessions.

Similarly, George Farkas has trained nonprofessional tutors in a program in Dallas that emphasizes word-attack and phonemic awareness. Farkas groups students in three stages: becoming letter and sound proficient, learning word families, and reading books.

All these projects achieve significant results.[9] By making use of special staff—Title I and special education teachers and aides and well-trained adult volunteers—any school can initiate an effective tutoring plan. However, the "Reading Recovery" specialists produce the most gains because of their intensive training and their extensive individual time with students.

Successful Reading
Programs in the Classroom

Several examples of what effective instruction could look like in the classroom have already been outlined. In addition, some of the newest reading series and several successful reading programs incorporate effective skills strands along the lines discussed earlier.

New Series

Some of the newest reading texts reflect a balanced approach and utilize the powerful research on effective reading strategies and best practices accumulated during the past decade. In one, for example, the first grade begins with two weeks of letter, sound, print awareness, and language review, primarily through game activities with students. Next, all students start working through approximately 100 lessons that provide enough basic letter/sound correspondences, sight words, word-attack skills, and language-structure knowledge to enable students to read trade books and a reading anthology that are part of the program. The authors have designed approximately five little books for each of these lessons. These books are not totally composed of soundable words, that is, the "cat sat on the mat" type. They illustrate how stories can be organized around skills lessons and still be interesting and use fascinating words; many of these stories use words such as *rhinoceros* along with words that are soundable and designed to reinforce skills lessons.

Some students work through the sequences rapidly, learn the concepts, and become ready for the trade books or basal stories in a few weeks. They quickly get the idea of and can recognize in print the letter/sound correspondence of a short *a* or even that the letter *c* can be soft or hard and what the pattern for that pronunciation is. However, most students take until December or January to reach this level. Others who have had little literacy preparation or have auditory, visual, or memory processing problems may take much longer. But every student must master this beginning sequence before moving ahead.

This program uses the instructional strategies of direct lesson introduction followed by guided reading of these specifically designed materials with the teacher, a partner, a parent, or individually. The teacher's role in working with a whole group or an individual is first to reinforce the lesson being taught, and second—and of even more importance—to get students thinking about how the various letter and letter combination, phonemic, and language and word structure systems work. As each lesson is learned, students become more able to learn the rest of these skills systems by themselves or with classmates through reading and answering questions about more sophisticated material.

Another crucial role for the teacher is to continually assess the reading progress of each student. One of the stories designed for each lesson is kept in reserve so that the words will not have been memorized, and it is then used to monitor progress by having the student read it to the teacher. The teacher determines if the error rate is small enough for the student to move on.[10] Sophisticated class management of the different strands and groups is necessary to free adequate time for the teacher to work with groups or conduct student conferences on a continual basis. In addition, teachers must learn to use simple error-analysis assessments of students reading to them for monitoring students' progress.

Finally, this program provides activities in encoding to reinforce decoding skills. Students write their own stories using words that reflect the correspondences being learned and they attempt to write and correctly spell dictated words related to their lessons and reading materials.

"Success for All"

Robert Slavin, a respected Johns Hopkins researcher, and his team have designed and implemented the "Success for All" program in more than 300 schools around the country. "Success for All" is a school-wide effort that has achieved remarkable success by substantially increasing the number of children who can read at grade level by the third grade in schools with high numbers of low-socioeconomic children or non-English speakers.[11]

The "Success for All" program is among the few reading approaches that gets proven results in tough schools because it is both comprehensive and provides a strong skills component. It includes

- Strands for skills development, literature, and writing activities
- Structural change at the school level
- A school-wide collective approach
- Integration of special programs into the overall school strategy
- Family and community support and engagement

- Availability of a sufficient number of books connected to lessons and at different levels
- An individual reading program
- Comprehension instruction
- Rapid intervention for children who are falling behind
- Continuous assessment of progress

This program also requires a commitment from the teaching staff and administration so it becomes a schoolwide endeavor. Finally, significant funds (usually from Title I) are invested in lowering class size for the reading period and providing tutors who work during the school day, teacher training, reading materials, an on-site project leader, and a community or family support person. Special program and categorical staff from federal and state funded programs actually coordinate their efforts with the overall reading strategies and work in tandem with the regular teaching staff. "Success for All" has cut the number of students requiring special education in half by teaching so many more children to read.

The other major reason the project produces results is that it assures that children learn the phonemic awareness, phonics, word attack, and other skills necessary to read. Schools in this program group students heterogeneously for most of the day, but reconstitute students in mixed-age groups based on common skill needs for a 90-minute reading and language skills period. Thus teachers can focus instruction on actual student needs. These classes are reorganized every 6 to 8 weeks to account for the progress students have made. The other language arts, including writing and editing and development of speaking and listening skills occur back in the regular, heterogeneously grouped classroom. "Success for All" is complemented by a recently development program called "Roots and Wings," which adds math, science, and social science to the "Success for All" reading, language arts, pre-kindergarten, kindergarten, tutoring, and family support programs.

"Reading Recovery"

Another example of these techniques is found in the strategies used by "Reading Recovery," a tutoring program originally developed by New Zealand psychologist and reading reform leader Marie Clay (see Clay, 1991). This program for lagging first graders uses a 30-minute-a-day individual tutoring strategy taught by a highly trained reading professional. However, the theory underlying the techniques in this one-on-one tutoring program can be adapted for use as the major strategy in the first-grade reading program.[12]

The tutor first evaluates which letters and sounds the student knows and then tailors instruction to extend that knowledge. The program has the student reread aloud a little book that he or she read the period before, and the tutor then introduces a new book. The tutor teaches the words that reflect the skills and strategies being learned, keeps track of mistakes, provides for subsequent activities with the words and word families, and has children write based on the story and read what they have written. An important part of instruction is teaching students how to monitor and self-correct their own reading, actively think about deciphering strategies, look at commonalities among words, see phrases and sentences, and learn to self-correct.

Deficiencies of Current Programs

Unlike the programs described above, very few instructional programs currently in use provide children with materials designed specifically to connect with systematic and sequenced skills development. In some cases, state, county, district, or university leaders are overtly or subtly antagonistic to the skills components, district policies discourage phonics teaching (Pressley & Rankin, 1994, p. 160), well-designed materials or teaching guides are not available, and new teachers and many instructional leaders are ill prepared in these research-grounded practices (Moats, 1994).

Often the only available follow-up reading materials are literature or trade books, meaning-based or literature-based basal texts, or the little books produced at various reading levels by a number of publishers, which, while interesting as stories, are not necessarily designed to be compatible with sequenced phonics lessons or even lessons based on a student's phonics needs.

The result is that many whole-language programs taught in schools or classrooms offer no organized skills and phonics instruction, except possibly in a catch-as-catch-can manner ("phonics on the fly"). This lack of a substantive skills and phonics program is disastrous for many children in light of the strong findings of research that show that the amount of time a student is engaged in phonics instruction is highly predictive of subsequent reading achievement and that a major distinction between good and poor readers is their knowledge of spelling patterns and their proficiency with spelling/sound translations.

As stressed earlier, a clear finding of research is that if students do not understand the idea of looking at the letters and patterns of letters in a word to trigger the meaning of the word very early in school, they quickly develop bad habits of guessing or flinching, which make reading more and more difficult (Stanovich, 1986). In addition, if the process of becoming automatic readers is drawn out too long, these students fall further and further behind their able-reading classmates who are reading greater and greater numbers of words and thinking about stories.

This failure to teach large numbers of students to read cannot be remedied by a sporadic, nonstrategic use of phonics instruction or the unproductive use of phonics worksheets. As the research demonstrates, effective skills instruction must be organized, sequenced, and comprehensive, while also being integrated with the overall English/Language Arts (ELA) program, so that students practice and overlearn these skills until they are automatic. At the same time, teachers must closely supervise and monitor progress.

Most distressing is the misleading advice offered by many popular reading manuals and training programs that tell teachers to deemphasize sound scanning of words and recommend that students initially not sound out the word or look at the letter patterns but look at pictures or guess from context. Even if the student guesses correctly, the word will be no easier to decode the next time it is encountered, although using context is helpful in resolving pronunciation ambiguities.

Even when the basic textbook contains some phonics instruction, schools often have adopted an unconnected skills program or the teachers have cobbled together some phonics lessons. The resulting phonics strand is either too peripheral, not intelligently integrated with other ELA instruction, or inconsistent with what is known about what works. Such ad hoc strategies do not produce the coherent, well-integrated ELA instructional program described by expert professionals.

In such situations, many teachers and students become frustrated at the lack of connection between basal readers or trade books and the phonics lesson, and many teachers start to spend less time directly teaching phonics and giving feedback while reading connected text. These teachers start relegating the phonics lessons, if any, to unsupervised seat work with phonics worksheets that are unconnected to individual needs or the rest of the language arts programs. Such weak instructional practices often fail to engage students.

Another problem with many basal-driven reading programs is that most basal texts are not organized around those few unfolding phonics lessons that are presented, but instead are based on students' abilities to read aloud. Consequently, slower students start at lower levels and are faced with easier stories. Most of the supplementary instruction such as these phonics lessons are then tied to how fast the student progresses through the stories in the basal text. The result is that the less well prepared the student is, the more slowly he or she will proceed through the materials, and the less he or she will learn about letter/sound correspondences and spelling patterns.

Compounding these problems is the unchallenging nature of the instruction that usually is available in schools with large numbers of low-achieving students. These students often encounter much easier texts than their suburban counterparts. In fact, some inner-city schools that organized their programs to enable their students to read materials comparable to the materials used at suburban schools found their students could read at suburban levels. Of course, these schools had to build in the skills instruction strands so that students could handle the books.

Poorly prepared students not only receive less phonics instruction but also are given little encouragement or opportunity to examine the structure of what they read, to reflect on aspects of its meaning, or to discuss its message. They do not learn self-monitoring techniques. Their supervised reading focuses on being accurate at oral reading and learning words, but very few of them actually become good readers (Adams, 1990, p. 417). Consequently, experts in reading instruction are encouraging publishers to introduce programs that do offer these preliminary skills strands along with properly designed reading materials and appropriate activities to teach them. More importantly, support must be provided to help all early elementary teachers learn how to be more effective literacy developers, understand the research, and become more adept at organizing a more flexible, comprehensive reading and language arts program.

Grouping Strategies

Each school is faced with the reality that children enter first grade with widely different literacy levels and backgrounds. Schools cannot simply pitch their programs at those who have high levels of literacy training and let the bottom third fend for themselves. Unfortunately, too many schools, although giving lip service to the slogan "all students can learn," in reality allow many to flounder without a successful plan for improvement. Conversely, schools should not run all students through the same lockstep curriculum at the same pace if some students can proceed faster or already know the material.

What to do? Most successful programs around the country have developed a form of organizing instruction around skills levels for part of the reading period. For example, some reading programs initially recommend the use of partners and other skills-organized groups in first grade, then suggest breaking children into research groups of four to six for second grade.

Another effective grouping method is demonstrated by "Success for All." That program uses the Joplin strategy of reconstituting the primary grades into mixed-age classes, each with a specified curriculum, for 90 minutes of reading instruction appropriate to that group. The rest of the day is spent in heterogeneous grade-level classes. The reading classes are reconstituted every 6 to 8 weeks based on student progress.

Other programs organize five to six groups within the first grade to correspond to what children are learning and are careful to move children to different groups when warranted. They conduct many whole-class and other heterogeneous group activities. All these programs provide additional time for independent reading of the designed materials or anything else the student wishes to read, writing and spelling, conferencing, and a variety of whole-language activities.

Which grouping strategy is appropriate for a particular school or class will depend on the mix of children, staff preferences, and how many groups and how much flexibility a teacher can handle. However, every first-grade teacher must deal with the issue of varied literacy levels and preparation, and make some flexible accommodation in order to be both fair and effective for all children.[13]

Determining Structure

A related question concerns whether or not every child should be sequenced through an organized program: Should reading programs assure that every child learns enough of the several cueing systems to become self-teaching, even though different students go through at different speeds, or should the teacher provide individualized help as needed in a tailored program?

In the two comprehensive reading programs just discussed, each student progressed through an organized sequence as fast as possible using grouping strategies. In "Reading Recovery," the teacher is highly experienced and there is a one-to-one teaching structure that enables the teacher to tailor instruction to the individual needs of the child.

However, even the students in "Reading Recovery" benefit from some explicit, organized sequencing. One of the most interesting research results that reinforces the need for a balanced approach is Iversen and Tunmer's (1993) finding that "Reading Recovery" produces a significantly greater impact when combined with extremely explicit instruction about phonology and decoding. The "Reading Recovery" program has been modified to incorporate these ideas. Marie Clay's *Reading Recovery: A Guidebook for Teachers in Training* (1993) places considerable emphasis on phonics and phonemic awareness and devotes substantial space in the sections on teaching procedures to letter identification (Sec. 3, p. 23), learning to look at print (Sec. 4, pp. 23-28), recognizing letters and sounds in their own writing (Sec. 5, p. 31), hearing and recording sounds in words (Sec. 6, pp. 32-35), linking sound sequence with letter sequence (Sec. 10, pp. 43-47), and taking words apart in reading (Sec. 11, pp. 47-51). The program now incorporates more extended phonemic awareness skills development in its daily sequence of activities with students.

There is no easy solution to this dilemma, but some general principles should assist teachers and schools. First, as noted above, there are a significant number of children, having either visual or auditory processing problems or few literacy experiences, who are going to need a long-term structured program. Second, every student needs some help in understanding how the total graphophonic, syntactic, and meaning system works, and each of them needs to be monitored for progress. Teachers who have a tremendous amount of experience will be able to juggle the large number of required strands and keep track of students in large classes, so that they can effectively tailor instruction as the professional tutors do. Many of these teachers are currently achieving fantastic results and should not change what they are doing; they are already successfully integrating skills with the other strands.

However, this way of teaching is very complex and constitutes a stretch for most primary teachers who do not have the vast experience and training necessary to effectively operate such a strategically run classroom. These less experienced teachers need a basic organized program that has enough flexibility to be adjusted to different groups of children and that can be tailored to the individual students as the teachers become more skilled in these strands (for a good discussion of this issue, see Pressley & Rankin, 1994, pp. 164-165). Professional development investments aimed at helping primary teachers move up the professional spectrum are crucial to increasing overall reading performance.

Notes

1. Exposure to print also contributes heavily to lexical knowledge (about 50% in both first and second grades—the more students read, the more words they understand). There is one major caution about exposure to print in the early grades. It only works if the student actually reads the words correctly—making mistakes in a large number of words doesn't help (Juel, 1994, pp. 122-125).

2. In response to those who disagree with using pseudowords out of context as an assessment, the vast majority of the research community maintains it is the best measure of decoding ability and actually replicates what a student faces in seeing a new word. As Share and Stanovich (1995b) write, "We know unequivocally that less-skilled readers have difficulty turning spellings into sounds. This processing deficit is revealed by the most reliable indicator of a reading disability: difficulty in rapidly and accurately reading pseudowords [citations omitted]" (p. 7). (Share is working on an additional test of decoding a word not read before by a particular student. The test provides unusual but soundable words in context, so that students can be assessed on the ability to generate plausible pronunciations and use context to select the right one [Share, 1995, p. 199].)

3. Juel (1994) cites similar results found by Lundberg in 1984 in Sweden, which starts children reading at age 7 (1 out of 8 chance for low phonemic first graders to become good readers by sixth grade), and by Marie Clay in New Zealand, which starts children reading at age 5.

> There is an unbounded optimism among teachers that children who are late in starting will indeed catch up. Given time, something will happen! In particular, there is a belief that the intelligent child who fails to learn to read well will catch up to his classmates once he has made a start. Do we have any evidence of accelerated progress in late starters? There may be isolated examples which support this hope, but correlations from a follow-up study of 100 children two to three years after school entry lead me to state rather dogmatically that where a child stood in relation to his age-mates at the end of his first year at school was roughly where one could expect to find him at 7:0 or 8:0. (Juel, 1994, p. 120)

4. According to Share and Stanovich (1995b), "A phonemically segmented lexicon (words placed in memory by their letter/sound patterns) in conjunction with the ability to supplement a not-yet-completed decoding with contextual information may permit the reader to achieve early 'closure' thereby easing the memory burden in decoding and reducing the likelihood that prior

sentence context will be lost as a consequence of slow and inefficient word identification."

5. For the point that just because students find it more and more difficult to memorize increasing numbers of words, they won't necessarily switch to an alphabetic decoding strategy, see Share and Stanovich (1995b), p. 20.

6. There is some dissent on whether word families should be taught as part of early beginning reading instruction. See the research cited pro and con by Share and Stanovich (1995a).

7. Juel (1994) used the Roper/Schneider oral test for phonemic awareness—early first grade; the Reading Comprehension Test of the Iowa Test of Basic Skills (appropriate for end of first grade); the WRAT reading subtest for word recognition; the Bryant Diagnostic Test of Basic Decoding Skills for cipher or decoding knowledge; the Spelling subtest of the ITBS for spelling or lexical knowledge; and the Metropolitan Readiness test for early first grade.

8. "Reading Recovery" is now exploring methods of applying their strategies to the regular classroom. For questions as to the cost-effectiveness of "Reading Recovery" and rebuttals to the criticism see Hiebert, E. H. (1994), Reading Recovery in the United States: What difference does it make to an age cohort? *Educational Researcher, 23* (9), 15-25; Lyons, C. A. and Beaver, J. (1995), Reducing retention and learning disability placement through Reading Recovery: An educationally sound cost-effective choice, in R. Allington and S. Walmsley, (Eds.) *No quick fix: Rethinking literacy programs in America's elementary schools* (pp. 116-136), New York: Teachers College Press; and the debate in *Reading Research Quarterly* starting with Pinnell, G. S., et al. (1994), Comparing instructional models for the literacy education of high risk first graders, *Reading Research Quarterly, 29*, 8-39; and the responses by Center, Y., et al. (1995), An evaluation of Reading Recovery, *Reading Research Quarterly, 30*, 240-260; Rasinski, T. (1995a), On the effects of Reading Recovery: A response to Pinnell, Lyons, DeFord, Bryk, and Seltzer, *Reading Research Quarterly, 30*, 264-270; Pinnell, G. S., DeFord, D. E., et al. (1995), Response to Rasinski, *Reading Research Quarterly, 30*, 272-275; and Rasinski, T. (1995b), Reply to Pinnell, DeFord, Lyons, and Bryk, *Reading Research Quarterly, 30*, 276-277.

9. "Success for All," Bob Slavin, Center for Research on Effective Schooling for Disadvantaged Students, Johns Hopkins University, 3505 N. Charles St., Baltimore, Maryland 21218, Tel: (410) 516-8806; "Reading Recovery," Gay Su Pinnell, Ohio State University, Tel: (614) 292-7875; Elfrieda Hiebert, Professor, University of Michigan School of Education, 610 E. University, 4202E SEB, Ann Arbor, Michigan 48109-1259; George Farkas, UTD Structured Tutoring Project, School of Social Science, University Texas at Dallas, Richardson, Texas 75083, Tel: (214) 690-2937. Connie Juel is Director of Studies in Learning to Read at the McGuffey Reading Center at the University of Virginia; Barbara Taylor is Chairperson, Department of Curriculum and Instruction in the College of Education at the University of Minnesota.

10. See Pinnell, G. S., DeFord, D. E., et al. (1995). "Reading Recovery" uses a running record in which a specialist or tutor has the student read a 100 to 150 word portion of text and keeps a running observation record of reading level, types of mistakes, correction strategies, and so on. The California

Learning Record is another example of keeping score. It is surprising how few elementary schools actually know where students are on a skills-development continuum or how many can read grade-appropriate materials. Standardized tests, usually given once a year, should only confirm what a teacher or the school already knows and are not available for weekly or monthly diagnostic and instructional purposes. Some of the commercial publishers' reading records are similar to, but simpler than, those in "Reading Recovery" and mainly give information on the amount and types of errors. The old rule of thumb was more than five mistakes a page and it's too hard.

11. The latest evaluations show an approximately one-half standard deviation more improvement than control groups in reading achievement (more with the bottom children) in the various "Success for All" sites (Slavin & Madden, 1995; Slavin, Madden, Dolan, & Wasik, 1995). Some "Success for All" programs are successfully using "Reading Recovery" as their tutoring component, for example, the Bakersfield Elementary School District in California. For information on the program or on the latest research verifying student achievement, contact Dr. Lawrence Dolan, Center for Research on Effective Schooling for Disadvantaged Students, Johns Hopkins University, 3505 N. Charles St., Baltimore, Maryland 21218, Tel: (410) 516-8806.

12. Gay Su Pinnell of Ohio State, who has promoted the "Reading Recovery" tutoring program in the United States from New Zealand, and Adria F. Klein, from San Bernardino State University and the 1995-1996 president of the California Reading Association, (909) 880-5605, are working on this issue of applying the techniques of "Reading Recovery" to the regular-reading first-grade program.

13. For an example, noted whole-language expert Dr. Terry Johnson of the University of Victoria recommends teacher-directed activities with students still working on a particular sound/letter correspondence (such as that found in a familiar rhyme) and having those who have mastered it move on to other activities such as independent reading (Johnson & Louis, 1990).

5

Reading Instruction for Middle First Grade to Upper Elementary Grades

A Book- and Story-Driven Strategy to Teach Skills

Once students possess the skills to read simple trade books, stories, children's magazines, and informational text from beginning anthologies or basal preprimers and primers, the most effective skills development strategy is to use these materials as the vehicle for extending the number of words that can be recognized automatically. If it takes several trials to move from sounding out a word to automatic recognition, then the more times a student reads a particular word, the more automatic he or she becomes. Most students become automatic with a word after recognizing it successfully 4 to 15 times. Some students, as they become more proficient, can recognize a word automatically after two or three tries. However, many learning disabled children need to read a word in context as many as 50 to 100 times before it becomes automatic.

As students learn to recognize more varied patterns of words, they establish more comprehensive letter/sound correspondences and spelling, syllable, word family, and word-root patterns in memory. They are then able to learn to recognize new words more quickly. Reading these materials also should sharpen decoding skills and enable students to learn new words and automatically recognize high-frequency words (many of which have irregular spelling/sound patterns) as well as the 300 word families which make up the 1,500 frequently used words in primary children's vocabularies (Adams, 1990, p. 321). These materials should be read as part of independent and guided reading programs aimed at extending reading capabilities and opening up doors of knowledge, enrichment, and joy for children. Direct teacher instruction should continue as a supplement to this strategy, especially in the area of the more complex decoding skills that depend on knowledge of advanced letter/sound correspondences, syllabication, word structure, spelling, and mechanics. Books should include both literary (stories based on narrative comprehension) and informational (based on expository comprehension such as in science, history, or biography) texts.

The books should also be read with partners or in groups reading a common text where content or even reading strategies can be discussed. Furthermore, the teacher should stress developing strategic word and text analytical skills such as awareness of language structure, recognizing word similarities, or understanding textual organization. Students should read large amounts of increasingly higher levels of materials (increasing the complexity of the vocabulary and conceptual load) to use and sharpen the growing number of skills they have learned. As in the pre-trade book stage, school or classroom programs can be legitimately organized in different ways to accomplish these tasks, but each successful program must deal with and solve a set of common problems.

First Principle:
Matching Books to Students' Levels

Classrooms should be filled with good children's literature appropriate to the various students' reading capabilities. This will take additional resources, but it is one of the best investments a school or district can make. Students who can decode well need more challenging materials and need to increase the amount they read, as the amount and level of reading becomes the strongest determinant of future growth. Juel (1994) found that for students scoring in the top quartile in reading comprehension at the end of first grade, almost all second-grade improvement in comprehension resulted from coverage of text. Conversely, as discussed above, if students have not yet mastered the sound/symbol system, coverage is less important than correctness.

All students should be reading just at the level where they can be extending their reading knowledge. If they are reading books and recognizing 98% to 100% of the words, they are not going to progress; conversely, if they cannot recognize at least 90% of the words and do not slow down enough to eventually read each word correctly, their reading time will not be effective.

Reading series offer a graduated variety of text. In addition, about a dozen publishers utilize a 1-20 rubric of difficulty for K-2 books. Books at the lower levels use simple sentence patterns, oral versus literary language, many supportive illustrations, and consistent placement of print. The upper-level materials use conventional stories, literary language, specialized vocabulary, written-language structures with oral language appearing in dialogue, challenging vocabulary, and few illustrations. These levels include familiar children's literature or informational books in areas such as science, history, and biography. Most students should reach these levels by the spring of first grade. "Reading Recovery," which uses these trade books, will enable a child to read 90 of these little books in a 6-week period (Pinnell, Lyons, DeFord, Bryk, & Seltzer, 1994).[1] Children eventually must read a tremendous amount of material, after they crack the code, if they are going to be grade-level readers by third grade and graduate from elementary school reading grade-appropriate materials—about 100 to 200 little books during the first grade and about 25 to 35 grade-equivalent fiction and nonfiction books a year starting in late first grade.

Once children can read more sophisticated classic and contemporary children's literature, nonfiction informational materials, and school texts in other subject areas, these materials can be used as the basis for assigned readings to generate more profound discussions about what has been read. Materials above students' reading levels should be read to them with follow-up discussions. Assignments in class can be oriented more to projects and activities that necessitate research or reading for a purpose. These types of activities should already be a staple of classroom organization.

Second Principle:
Frequent Evaluation of Students' Reading

If organizing a reading program to encourage students to read diverse texts is going to be an effective instructional strategy, it is essential that most of what students read is challenging enough to develop their automatic word recognition, vocabulary, and skills, but not so hard that students become frustrated. Student background knowledge plays a role in this equation. As stated, a good rule of thumb is that if students cannot automatically recognize at least 90% of the words, they will become frustrated; if they sail through, recognizing 98% of the words, they are missing an opportunity to extend their word learning. (This formula does not mean students should never read an interesting book if it is too hard or too easy; rather, that a steady diet of either extreme will cause problems.) Students should be recognizing approximately 95% of the words automatically, which means they are decoding (in the sense of figuring out) about 1 word in 20. This requires teachers to keep tabs on how each student is doing. Frequent conferencing, having the child read to the teacher, and other similar techniques are important components of any successful reading class.

Many existing practices for grouping violate this principle of ensuring that the reading materials are appropriate to the child's needs. First, assignment to large reading groups or whole-class instruction means that only some children have appropriate materials. Most often, the group is paced by the best readers and the others do not have a chance to achieve correctness with each word (Juel, 1994, p. 127).

Second, districts and principals often pressure teachers to cover an established amount of material. Groups may start slowly in a preprimer but accelerate and lose children. In Juel's study, the pace speeded up when the group reached the primer stage, and by February students were recognizing only 66% of the words. Rather than slow down, reread, or use similar techniques, the group simply forged ahead. By June, word recognition was still only 69% and reading comprehension was only at the 29th percentile. (Recall that if basal texts were read at a slower rate with at least 90% correctness, comprehension scores were way above average [Juel, 1994, p. 127].)

Third, in most classes few shifts occurred between groups even if a student was reading with extremely high accuracy. Unfortunately, second-grade placement often was made not on ability, but on a student's last reading-group assignment. Most effective programs reconstitute reading groups every 6 weeks or so.

Finally, allowing much free reading results in students picking books significantly below or above their reading level, and considerable effort on the part of the teacher is necessary to keep children in the right books. In a recent research report, Ronald Carver and R. Leibert (1995) found that a significant percentage of the books picked as grade-appropriate material for fifth graders were actually at third-grade level (p. 43).

In summary, when readers read easy books, they do not encounter the new vocabulary and more sophisticated ideas necessary for growth. Conversely, when poor readers pretend to read, or any readers continue to struggle through books significantly above their abilities, they will become frustrated—unless, of course, their proficiency accommodates quickly to the harder material by their learning the specific vocabulary and ideas of the topic covered by the book.

One of the most needed tools for teachers is a uniform standard for determining the grade level of a book—not as an average in a nationally normed test but as a measure of difficulty appropriate for a given grade. Until recently, teacher judgment and library lists with broad ranges (e.g., third to fifth grade) had to suffice. A major breakthrough has occurred with the development of the Lexile Sysem by Metametrics in Morrisville, North Carolina. They have created a proportional scale and software that can place a book on the scale based on the number of infrequent words occurring and the amount of internal text references (phrases and clauses). They have ranked over 3,000 children's and adults' books and materials. For example, *Cat in the Hat* is ranked 200; *Goodnight, Moon* is 300; *Charlotte's Web* is 800; *The Adventures of Tom Sawyer* is 1,000; *USA Today,* 1,100; *The Wall Street Journal,* 1,400. The highest level is George Washington's Inaugural Address, at 1,700. Reading at a 500 lexile level means that a student can get 75% of comprehensive questions correct on material at that level. (The scale is logarithmic, so that being at 500 means that a student will get only 50% of comprehensive questions right at the 700 level, and this relationship holds throughout the scale. The Lexile Analyzer software will rank any book or any student.)

Continued Letter/Sound, Spelling, and Decoding Support

As discussed previously, students in middle first grade are still at different levels of proficiency in decoding, phonemic awareness, and word-attack and strategic skills. Teachers will need to provide ongoing support in these areas until the students have learned the letter/sound system completely and have mastered more complex decoding and word-attack skills. For most students, this should occur by the end of second grade. Instruction in spelling, which also contributes significantly to reading improvement, should continue throughout the elementary years.

Syllables and Word Roots

Marcia Henry, Carrol Moran, and Robert Calfee make the important point that one of the prime difficulties of reading English as words become more complicated is the complex nature of breaking words into parts (see Henry, Calfee, & La Salle, 1989, p. 155 et seq.; Moran & Calfee, 1993, pp. 210-212).

William Nagy, in a presentation at the 1995 American Educational Research Association conference, reinforced the point that English becomes increasingly morphologically complex in the texts used in upper grades. He noted that students must learn huge numbers of complex words and that one of the difficulties they face is the tendency of many word roots to change spelling and pronunciation in different word forms. In English, the word root (or morpheme) that carries the meaning—for example, *nature, natural, denatured*—is often different than the syllable. The historical creation of English becomes important in understanding the structure of words because the language of each historical contributor to English has its own peculiar pattern of letter/sound correspondences, syllabication, morphemes, and word generation.[2]

For example, words with an Anglo-Saxon etymology are the common, everyday words, such as *sister* or *railroad,* used in ordinary situations. Many words, such as *football,* were added to the English vocabulary by combining two other words. Words derived from Latin and French are more technical, formal, and literary such as *manuscript, facilitate,* or *international.* Many words were created by adding prefixes or suffixes to a word root that usually cannot stand alone, such as *traction.* Greek-derived words, such as *biology* or *television,* are found primarily in technical fields and are specialized.

In summary, it is also important to help students become aware of the more complex syllabication patterns as words become more multisyllabic. According to reading experts, students need to learn about the underlying structure of words in our language to become proficient readers and writers. Knowing the different patterns and roots becomes essential as material increases in difficulty. A proficient reader needs to possess rapid access to potential letter/sound, syllable, onset/rime, and word-root patterns to help break up and decipher any particular word.

Skills Development

Grammar, Usage, Composition, Mechanics, Syllabication, and Text Structure

From first grade on, reading and language arts programs need a strand of continuing skills development for grammar, usage, and composition; mechanics (such as capitalization and punctuation); syllabication, prefixes, suffixes, and derivatives such as *ing* and *ed;* and sentence, paragraph, and text structure (story structure, poems, newspaper articles, editorials, etc.). These skills should not be de-emphasized in the mistaken belief that they can be learned only in context of writing or that teaching skills hampers writing. Most textbooks contain material to teach these skills.

The controversy arises over how best to teach them. As in decoding, there must be a sequenced plan of direct instruction of these skills. Similarly, an overemphasis on teaching of discrete skills—for example, through the heavy use of worksheets isolated from use in natural writing—will not be very effective in improving writing or reading. Some combination of organized, direct skills instruction; numerous opportunities to practice in natural writing; mini-lessons and reteaching when needed; and insistence that final drafts be correct seems the best approach. Finally, an assessment system is needed to ascertain who has mastered the skill and who has not. Those who are not proficient in a particular skill must be given further assistance.

The development of other essential skills—spelling, writing, vocabulary and word choice, specific comprehension strategies, listening, discussion, and oral expression—are discussed in the next three chapters.

SUMMARY

Systematic and sequenced instruction in skills is not a drill or worksheet program, but an integrated approach that combines direct teaching, reading materials designed to reinforce the concept, and metacognitional and strategic assistance. It should also include plenty of practice in a variety of reading and writing situations until the particular skill is overlearned, and the use of some manipulative or game strategies to further reinforce the skill.

Instruction should stress word-attack skills, thinking about whether the word makes sense, and other strategic and phonics techniques. It should take place initially while reading engaging stories that are designed to bolster the systematic development of word families and other key skills such as syllabication, mechanics, and so on. Later, instruction can use different levels of trade books and stories in textbooks and be supplemented by activities that reinforce learning, such as word play, activities with words, and blending practice. Skills instruction should be organized, occupy a significant portion of reading instruction, and be integrated into a comprehensive language arts strategy.

Notes

1. Three other programs observed by Pinnell et al. (1994) resulted in students reading only an average of 4, 16, and 31 books during the same period.

2. For three fascinating accounts of the historical basis of the creation of English and the many linguistic streams that feed into it, see Bryson (1990), Claiborne (1983), and Crystal (1995).

6

Spelling, Beginning Writing, and Vocabulary

Spelling

Spelling and beginning writing are essential components of any successful reading program in kindergarten, first grade, and beyond. As mentioned earlier in the kindergarten section, learning to print letters obviously helps a student recognize them. Beginning writing and spelling activities that have students attempt to translate oral words to written words (encoding, which is the converse of decoding) help reinforce the letter/sound system. Subsequently, an organized spelling program is essential for first through eighth grades and should aim toward making students good spellers.

Temporary or Invented Spelling Issues

In many schools, students begin writing before the formalized reading program starts and writing becomes a powerful tool in developing skills and knowledge about reading. "Invented" or "temporary" spelling is a technique that allows students to approximate the letter and patterns of letters that represent a given sound and so permits the construction of more advanced writing connected to student interests.

91

It is a helpful technique for encouraging students to write, and it pays off in increased writing volume and more elaborate stories, which in turn encourage children to think more about what they are writing than do traditional techniques. Temporary spelling also helps with understanding the phonics principle.

Adams (1990) points out that the payoff for students who have had ample experience with temporary spelling is in spelling growth and reading fluency (p. 383), but cautions that writing using temporary spelling cannot replace instruction and practice in reading and word recognition. She argues that direct instruction in word analysis and consonant blending is a necessary complement to children's independent orthographic intuitions (pp. 378-388).

The issue of how best to correct temporary or approximated spelling is tricky and controversial. On the one hand, in preschool and kindergarten, invented spelling is a natural stage in developing the ability to write and spell, and teachers should allow room for natural child development and approximation. After kindergarten, writing (encoding) is used not just for expression, but also as a powerful technique to help children learn the letter patterns necessary for automatic decoding. At this stage, developmental spelling becomes an important diagnostic tool for determining how much progress the student has made in learning the sound/symbol system and what further instruction needs to occur. For example, writing *sumtime* for *sometime* shows good phonic skills and understanding of English spelling patterns, whereas *smtym* is much less developed.

Feedback also should be given to students about the correct spelling of the words not yet spelled correctly so that they do not incorrectly learn letter patterns they are trying to assimilate in reading. Marie Clay (1991) suggests that parents and teachers should provide correct spellings when acting as a recorder (such as retyping a student's story in correct English). Some whole-language purists advocate refusing to answer a child even if he or she asks for the correct spelling, but this policy seems misguided (Adams, 1990, p. 388). A good compromise position is to acknowledge that temporary spelling is a useful tool in teaching writing and in diagnosing how well children understand the phonemic system, but as children get older, and especially in that crucial period in first grade when they are learning to read, some form of modeling the correct pattern or building on the approximation seems important. By middle to late first grade, words in final drafts should be spelled correctly.

Importance of Spelling

According to Marilyn Adams (1990) and others (see, for example, Woloshyn & Pressley, 1995), an organized spelling program in which children learn to spell large numbers of words correctly is one of the most productive, and most neglected, strategies in helping children learn to read (p. 375 et seq.).

There is a growing consensus that spelling is also a powerful strategy in helping students communicate through writing. Donald Graves (1994), one of the most respected leaders in the writing reform movement, makes the following comments about this subject in his recent book, *A Fresh Look at Writing:*

> Spelling does matter. It matters far more than we in the profession realize. Spelling, probably more than any other aspect in the school curriculum, is used to mark social status. . . . Spelling matters for another reason. Children who initially write down words using inventions or temporary spellings are establishing their learning habits and attitudes towards words and writing. As arbitrary as spelling may appear, specific things should be taught and certain attitudes established. It is not enough for the writer to know what the text says. As Mary Ellen Giacobbe points out, the reader needs to know as well. Writing is communication. (pp. 255-256)

Teaching Spelling

What is at issue is how best to teach spelling: whether there should be direct instruction in spelling and what method should be used—assignment and assessment of lists of words, or spelling assignments stemming from writing and reading? Marilyn Adams reviewed the literature on spelling in her 1990 work, *Beginning to Read,* and Vera Woloshyn and Michael Pressley reviewed the spelling research in their 1995 update, *Cognitive Strategy Instruction That REALLY Improves Children's Academic Performance* (see also a good review of recent spelling research in Topping, 1995). For the most part they all reach similar conclusions about the salient facts of spelling instruction. The ideas in the following section on spelling are from Adams (1990), pp. 388-404, and Woloshyn and Pressley (1995), pp. 116-152.

Woloshyn and Pressley agree with Graves and Adams that spelling is important as a sign of literacy and that it is connected to good reading. Motivation to spell well is important and being a good speller is within almost everyone's reach, since spelling vocabularies of only about "3,000 words are sufficient for fluent and intelligent communication for adults" (Woloshyn & Pressley, 1995, p. 116). Fifty words account for half of written material and 1,000 words account for 86%. A small number of words—about 300—account for more than half the words children misspell in their writing.

According to Woloshyn and Pressley (1995), a marked shift in spelling instruction should occur in late first or early second grade. By that time, children should have progressed from using only salient sounds to a phonetic phase in which they try to match a letter for each sound and are now ready for the more complicated orthographic learning necessary to become proficient at spelling. To become good spellers, they must graduate from relying only on sounding-out strategies to the more complex spelling-pattern stage based on orthographic patterns and word roots and incorporating a variety of more complex strategies in learning to spell a word (p. 117).

Adams (1990) concurs. She states that good spelling does not stem from understanding the pronunciation of words. Students can understand spelling-to-sound rules very well, but these rules do not work in reverse. The letter *f* quite reliably symbolizes the sound /f/. The sound /f/ can be spelled as *f, ff, ph,* or *gh* and the /ur/ sound can be represented as *bird, father, urn,* or *burr.* Although few rules or patterns determine which words belong with which family, and each must be individually learned and placed in their right families, there are a limited number of patterns that apply. Good spellers use visual or orthographic knowledge to connect an individual word to an existing pattern (Adams, 1990, p. 394), and they use a variety of techniques such as breaking words into units (not necessarily syllables) and trying to visualize how they look, breaking the word into smaller parts and spelling the part by analogizing it to a known pattern, and using spelling rules (Woloshyn & Pressley, 1995, p. 118). For most children, then, becoming a good speller depends on a systematic program using a variety of techniques to place in long-term memory large numbers of words that are governed by these arbitrary and sophisticated spelling patterns.

Poor spellers do not visually recognize word spellings completely or quickly enough to use any but the simplest and most salient orthographic features in their identification. In contrast, good spellers visually recognize a complex set of regular and irregular spelling patterns and can link them to pronunciations effortlessly and accurately. Unfortunately, many poor spellers become poor readers in later grades because they do not have a complete enough representation of spelling patterns in their memory and thus cannot process individual letters of words with the ease necessary for fluent reading. If students cannot be persuaded to pay more attention to less familiar orthographic patterns, neither their reading nor their spelling will improve (Adams, 1990, p. 394).

If the solution to widespread poor spelling that affects reading ability is to install huge numbers of words in long-term memory, how best should this be accomplished? It turns out that looking at a word in print is a much superior method of learning spelling patterns than hearing it spelled. Also, teaching children word structures or morphology—*fat, fatter,* and *fattest* all stem from *fat*—is an important component of literacy instruction. One would think that pointing out morphology patterns would help spelling. Woloshyn and Pressley (1995) think it does; Adams (1990, p. 400) has some questions and states that the reverse is probably true: Knowing spelling most likely helps children learn morphology.

All three agree, however, that the most successful method of teaching students to spell is for teachers to habitually encourage students to look at spelling patterns of the vocabulary words they want them to learn. Teachers can write them on the board or point to them on a page. Then students must make several attempts to recall the spelling and write the word correctly until it is learned (placed in long-term memory). According to Woloshyn and Pressley (1995), students must be taught several memory strategies and how to use these strategies in learning to spell. Finally, writing activities, self-correcting, editing, and testing strategies using vocabulary words are essential to reinforce spelling.

Which Strategies?

Preliminarily, according to Adams (1990) and Woloshyn and Pressley (1995), a strong empirical finding of research is that many children will not learn to spell unless instructed. Sufficient time must be devoted to spelling—about 60 to 75 minutes a week, or 15 minutes a day. More time than that is not effective. However, current estimates are that 30% to 80% of spelling time is wasted on irrelevant administrative or pedagogical activities such as correcting workbooks (Woloshyn & Pressley, 1995, p. 119).

These researchers make several forceful points about instruction, as follows:

- Make sure students are ready to learn from an organized spelling program (they need phonics, print awareness, a basic ability to write some words, and reading at late first- or early second-grade level).
- Stress motivation and pride in spelling correctly.
- Devote 12 to 15 minutes a day to instruction (or 60 to 75 minutes a week).
- Limit use of phonics techniques by supplementing with more orthographic techniques to learn patterns starting in late first and early second grade.
- Teach spelling rules that apply to a large number of words and have only a few exceptions (e.g., rules about the addition of suffixes and inflected endings such as *bake/baking, bake/baker, fly/flies, baby/babies, play/playful,* and *run/running;* when to capitalize; how to use apostrophes; rules about the letter *s* and plurals; abbreviations; *q* is followed by *u;* no English words end in *v; i* before *e* except after *c*).
- Present spelling words in lists rather than in context because students then attend to the pattern behind the word; lists should be organized by similar sounds or sound patterns.
- Study spelling words as whole units versus syllabified forms.
- Teach students to pronounce words clearly (choc-*o*-late).
- Use the test-study-test method versus the study-test method. (One of the strongest research findings is that testing children first so that they do not waste their time on words they already know is very effective; subsequently, the final exam tests both unknown and known words.)
- Have students monitor their own spelling progress through self-correction of tests (one of the most effective learning-to-spell techniques), editing, and computer work.
- Individualize spelling instruction.
- Teach imaging, analogy, and morphological strategies and how to use combinations of strategies.

- Have students practice using words in their writing and continue to be tested on words they studied previously for reinforcement. (pp. 120-149)

Which Words?

Several strategies are available to help students remember the spellings of a large number of words. First, since many of the beginning word families are regular, learning to spell those is relatively easy. Practicing spelling those words and using them in writing should accompany learning to read them. Especially in the first grade, spelling and writing dictated words should be connected to the phonics lessons being learned. The recurring irregular words—such as *were, water, also,* and *too* or *two*—should be memorized initially. After that there should be a systematic introduction and learning of sufficient words to correspond to the increasing vocabulary in reading materials. These should be organized by word families and systematic attention should be given to spelling demons that trouble large numbers of students. Misspelled words in students' writing can also be included as words to learn.

One key point is to provide enough reinforcement so that the word is firmly placed in long-term memory. Much is known about how to memorize. Unless a pattern already exists, it takes five to eight conscious, separate attempts to memorize something before it is learned for good; most of the time it is not learned. For example, most people continue to look up telephone numbers they use all the time. They just have not forced themselves to implant the number in long-term memory by reading it and trying to recall it several times. Further, if they never use the number they will forget it again, so it is important to reinforce what has been learned. While many words do have patterns, it is necessary to remember visually or mentally which pattern is right through conscious recall.

It is also important that teachers establish standards for correct final drafts of written assignments. Many writing programs so concentrate on the expressiveness of the initial drafts and are so careful not to squelch creativity that they forget the importance of requiring a polished and correct final product.

In summary, a good spelling program after the first grade will help organize a long-term memorization project for each student that systematically presents the words he or she uses or reads. The secret is to screen out those words that can already be spelled so that the student can concentrate each week on memorizing 7 to 10 words he or she cannot spell. Giving all students a common list of words each week is easy to organize, but it is inefficient. It does not ensure that words that were missed last week actually get learned, and it does not help screen out words that students already know so they can concentrate on words they do not know.

Having students write natural text using a rich vocabulary also gives continual practice and reinforcement for spelling, as does reading large amounts of material. However, students attempting to comprehend text tend not to pay attention to the details of complicated spelling patterns. Rereading will help, as will presenting students with words isolated from text, so there is no comprehension pressure to divert their attention (Adams, 1990, p. 397). Periodically, a way should be provided of getting students to review what they have learned, such as preparation for a spelling bee. The number of words covered each year should aim at almost total mastery of grade-level words by the end of eighth grade.

Beginning Writing

Connie Juel (1994) also examined the acquisition of writing in her study of low-income primary students (pp. 25-49). In reporting on writing research, she delineates the correlational sequence.

In first grade, she concludes, writing depends two thirds on the ability to spell words and one third on the quality and ability to produce story ideas, including planning, reflecting, and revising. By second grade, these two factors have reversed. Spelling ability is determined by two main factors in first grade—cipher (or decoding) knowledge and lexical or memorized spelling patterns for that word. Both these factors decrease by second grade, but still account for the majority of writing ability. Thus first-grade writing is affected by some of the same factors as reading. (In first grade, writing ability is highly correlated with word recognition, and reading comprehension becomes increasingly correlated with writing ability as the grades progress.) It is apparent not only that learning to read helps learning to write and vice versa but that low phonemic awareness that inhibits learning cipher knowledge also stymies writing growth.

As described previously, students who learn to approximate spellings through temporary spelling will make predictable errors based on their incipient phonic and phonemic knowledge. Children who must rely solely on remembering letter patterns through lexical knowledge, without benefit of any phonemic help, produce much less sophisticated approximations.

Juel (1994) and her fellow researchers devised a nine-point writing scale and then did backward mapping similar to what they did in reading by looking at which factors seemed to make a difference. Poor writers either spelled poorly or generated poor ideas. If a child was a poor reader, the odds were that the child would also be a poor writer by the fourth grade, and the correlation between reading ability and writing ability increased each year. This seemed partly explained by the influence of oral storytelling ability—a major determinant of the idea side of writing—and exposure to expository (nonfiction) text. No poor reader could score higher than 4 out of 9 levels on a basically expository fourth-grade prompt.

Interestingly, all first graders scored about the same on Juel's writing scale measure, but the good readers who encountered increasingly sophisticated stories as they were exposed to print increased significantly in the next three grades, whereas the poor readers stayed flat. As a result, a significant gap opened up by fourth grade. Juel (1994) explains that early reading ability affects the desire to read, which affects the amount of exposure to print, which affects later reading, writing, and speaking ability (p. 48).

Vocabulary

The automatic recognition of an increasing number of vocabulary words is key to developing the ability to understand text at increasing levels of difficulty. As stated earlier, the best way of extending vocabulary is to read a large amount of text.

In addition, there should be a vocabulary strand in any quality reading program. Rather than teach words directly—they are best learned through reading—it should teach how to analyze words (look at their internal structure such as word roots and families), the structure of the English language, synonyms, and strategies to figure out a word from context. (These context clues differ from the earlier debate about whether a student can decode a word from context. In the current discussion, the student can decode or say the word; he or she does not yet understand what the word means.) In addition, programs that foster conscious attention to the subtleties of word use and also utilize word games are extremely productive. For a good summary, see the work of Susan Watts and Michael Graves on fostering word consciousness and Judy Scott's word and phrase borrowing techniques (Scott, Hiebert, & Anderson, 1994; Watts & Graves, 1995).

One of the most grievous deficiencies in most elementary classrooms is the absence of any formalized vocabulary attention. Several of the better vocabulary programs are listed in *Teaching Vocabulary to Improve Reading Comprehension* (1988) by William Nagy, *The Nature of Vocabulary Acquisition* (1987) by Margaret G. McKeown and Mary E. Curtis, the chapter on vocabulary in *Cognitive Strategy Instruction that REALLY Improves Children's Academic Performance* (1995) by Michael Pressley and Linda Lysynchuk, and *The Vocabulary Conundrum*, by Richard Anderson and William Nagy (1992).

According to these sources, an organized vocabulary instruction should include the following:

- An individualized reading program for each student that covers a large amount of text
- Reading to and discussing ideas and books with students
- Teaching word roots, different structures of words from the different languages that make up English, and other internal context clues (English is made up of Anglo-Saxon, French, Latin, Greek, and, now, international words. Marcia K. Henry, Robert C. Calfee, and Robin Avelar La Salle have thoroughly reviewed the teaching of the structure and history of words in the 1989 Yearbook of the National Reading Conference and Carrol Moran and Bob Calfee's *Comprehending Orthography* discussed in Chapter 4.)
- Using definitions to help students process the word (Looking words up in the dictionary is a weak strategy because the definitions are misleading; revising the definition into clearer language is much more effective.)
- Learning to use external context clues
- Semantic mapping and synonyms
- Using the best word in a writing situation
- Processing new words in multiple ways

7

Comprehension and Assessment

As mentioned earlier, strong literature (including nonfiction), independent reading, and comprehension strands are essential to any effective reading program. According to Richard Anderson of the Center for the Study of Reading at the University of Illinois (personal communication, April 1995), there are three major strategies to teach comprehension:

1. Reading a lot
2. Strategic reading
3. Deep discussions about books or articles

Reading comprehension initially depends almost exclusively on students' ability to automatically read words that are already in their speaking vocabulary and that represent familiar concepts through the rapid use of the orthographic, phonemic, semantic, and syntactic cueing systems. As discussed earlier, after readers become more fluent, listening comprehension, vocabulary, informational and conceptual knowledge about the world, and reading strategies become more important to reading comprehension. Even more importantly, instruction should include an organized component with individualized reading, strategic reading, and discussion strands.

Finally, in the early primary grades, reading to students, having them retell the stories, and discussing issues in those books can be done at levels significantly higher than students' existing reading levels.

The Read-a-Lot Strategy

The best strategy for developing comprehension is for teachers to require students to read a significant amount of age-appropriate quality material. *"Reading a lot" is one of the most powerful methods of increasing fluency, vocabulary, and comprehension, and becoming educated about the world* (Shany & Biemiller, 1995; Stanovich, 1993).

Growth in comprehension depends on reading a substantial number of words each year from a variety of high-quality children's literature and informational texts such as favorite stories, children's newspapers, science and history books, biographies, and so on. One of the New Standards Project's performance standards expects each student to read 25 grade-appropriate books from accepted library lists during each year of elementary, middle, and high school. A goal of 25 to 35 grade-appropriate fiction and nonfiction books from accepted lists seems right for most children.

There are two main rationales for this recommendation. First, comprehension cannot improve unless the student is increasing the number of words that can be recognized and understood automatically. Shu, Anderson, and Shang (1995) cite numerous studies show that a high correlation between vocabulary growth and increases in reading comprehension (pp. 76-86). Getting meaning from text depends on first deciphering a word until it is conscious, understanding the concept embodied in that word, and then relating that word to other words in the sentence. At first, students know most of the words encountered in text; they need to recognize that the letters on the page represent a word they already know. Soon after the early primary years, however, students need to learn a substantial number of new words if they are to understand grade-level material. These words usually are the key to understanding the meaning of a passage. Eventually, students will need to learn to automatically recognize these words to stay at grade level.

Average fifth-grade students encounter about 36,000 new words per year in the course of their reading. If readers must slow down to sound out a substantial number of words in a passage or, worse, if they miss the meaning of key words, they will not be able to attend to the meaning of what is being read. Thus they need to learn the meaning and automatic recognition of large numbers of new words each year. Since students remember about 5% of new words encountered in context, an average student will learn only about 1,800 words a year, not enough to keep up with needed vocabulary development. They must read more text if they are to extend their vocabulary (see Adams, 1990, p. 149; Anderson, 1992; Juel, 1994, p. 120; Krashen, 1993; Pressley & Lysynchuk, 1995, p. 102).

Students should be learning approximately 3,000 to 4,000 words a year throughout their upper elementary careers if they are to be literate adults. Currently, only one of every five children reads enough to achieve this level.

Thus, by the fifth grade, if elementary students want to make grade-level progress, they should be reading more than 1.1 million words a year of outside-school reading (25 to 35 books or the equivalent), which should take 15 to 30 minutes a night; this is in addition to the 1.7 million words in school text. Instead of reading the necessary 2.8 million words, the average fifth grader reads only about 900,000. Current U.S. students read much less than they once did—which is one reason reading scores are dropping—and much less than students in other countries. Although teaching vocabulary strategies (word families, scaffolding, etc.) helps retention rates, the vast majority of new words *can be learned only through reading*. To reach these levels, students need to read the recommended 25 to 35 books a year after the first grade.

A second reason that reading itself is the best way to improve comprehension is that reading a large amount of material provides students with a broad and deep encounter with ideas, concepts, and knowledge. This, in turn, helps improve their ability to comprehend. By reading a variety of age-appropriate material from accepted lists, students should become more educated about the personal, social, literary, political, ethical, and scientific worlds. Becoming more literate is desirable on its own merits, but because background knowledge has a major influence on comprehension, being well-read contributes significantly to the ability to comprehend a wider and more difficult amount of written material.

Individualized Reading Program

Schools need to develop an individual reading program, with a targeted number of books to read from acceptable lists, for each student. Ideally, each student will keep a record of what has been read, and the schools will establish a mechanism to determine that books have actually been read.

This strategy requires a significant number of books to be available in the classroom and school library. Unfortunately, very few schools have an organized individual reading program geared to specific targets with a credible way of checking to see if the book was read, although many schools do stress individual reading and display the books that students read. As a result, under the current system only a few students read enough to reach the levels necessary for continued development.

Requiring a specific number of books to be read and keeping track of them is probably the easiest and most productive reading program a school could undertake. Parental involvement in the process—setting time aside for reading at home, discussing the book with a child, looking at the reading record—can greatly assist in attaining this goal. There is no excuse for not instituting this program in every elementary school in the country.

Strategic Reading

The second comprehension strategy is to develop metacognitional skills: connecting what is about to be read to what the student already knows, outlining, asking internal questions about the material, explaining what has been read to someone, or writing something about it. A powerful example of this strategy is Reciprocal Teaching, a program developed by A. L. Brown and A. S. Palincsar (1984), that uses techniques of guided instruction to help students generate questions, summarize, clarify word meanings or confusing text, and make predictions. A recent review of these techniques showed significant gains of about a third of a standard deviation on standardized tests and .88 standard deviation on researcher-designed comprehension tests (the research reviewed included older students) (Rosenshine & Meister, 1994).

Pressley and his colleagues have also thoroughly discussed the benefit of strategic reading for the development of comprehension ability and the ability to extract the gist or macrostructure of what has been read (Pressley et al., 1992; Pressley & Rankin, 1994, p. 159; Pressley, Symons, McGoldrick, & Snyder, 1995). They advocate programs for Grades 3 through 8 (some strategies are appropriate in earlier grades) in which teachers use strategies to assist children in making mental associations between what they have read and their own personal experiences, interpreting them, and creating summaries of what they found important in the text. An individual strategy usually takes about 10 hours to teach. Not every strategy needs to be taught to every child, although each child needs a basic set.

The following are examples of strategies:

- summarization (includes such activities as substituting categories for lists of items, integrating a series of events with a descriptive action term, and selecting or inventing a topic sentence, so that a student can explain in his or her own words what happened or the structure of an argument);
- constructing mental imagery of what is being read;
- constructing questions, answering questions, look-backs;
- learning story grammar;
- activating prior knowledge; and, of most importance,
- the strategic use of a set of these tools.

These strategies are used in small group discussions about what has been read, in which students share ideas and support points with information from the text. Students also use what they have read as a basis for writing (Brown, Pressley, Schuder, & Van Meter, 1994). Most other successful programs, such as "Reading Recovery" and "Success for All," rely on these strategies.

Discussion of Books

The third comprehension strategy, which unfortunately is all too rare in most American classrooms, is the use of numerous deep intellectual discussions, either orally or in writing, about the meaning and significance of what the author has written. According to a growing number of scholars and practitioners, a steady diet of intellectual conversations about important ideas and events is the most powerful stimulant to increasing reading comprehension (see the rest of Chapter 7 for supporting documentation). In the earlier grades, this strategy can be enhanced by the teacher reading aloud to the class material that is too difficult for them to read and then using it as the basis for the discussion.

Ideas Behind Discussions

Arthur Applebee and Judith Langer[1] have been championing reader response strategies based on in-depth discussion of students' initial responses to a particular text (see Applebee, 1992a, 1992b, 1994; Langer, 1992, 1993, 1994, in press). What these pioneers advocate is remarkably consistent with expert recommendations in learning strategies in math and science, which are based on sophisticated teacher responses to how students are thinking about a problem.

Some advocates have taken this position too far, in part abetted by Langer's earlier writing that seemed to neglect the importance of understanding the author's message—a stance she has recently clarified. These radical constructivists claim that the content of what is read is unimportant and not very useful in educating our children because, they argue, most meaning is idiosyncratic and based in the reader's experience. That claim seems farfetched, for there are enduring childhood favorites that appeal to almost every child, and the wisdom of the past enshrined in many classics is useful knowledge that can instruct large numbers of diverse students in how to live their lives. Most children love *Charlotte's Web* and are moved by *The Diary of Anne Frank,* and every potential citizen can learn about the central principles of our democracy from *The Declaration of Independence.*

Anderson (1992), Applebee (1992a, 1992b, 1994), and Langer (1992, 1993, 1994, in press) advocate a more balanced position. They contend that there are two major types of reading comprehension: narrative or literary, in which the story is key, and expository or discursive, such as the logical arguments made in science or social studies. Strategies that invoke an individual response are especially effective in deepening discussions of books. Engagement in a story often provides the vehicle for more open-ended personal responses or, in Langer's words, "exploring a horizon of possibilities" (in press,

p. 37) where the interpretation of text keeps changing as deeper analysis and reader reaction interact. In addition, literary readings are one of the best vehicles for teaching students how to deal with the nuance, ambiguity, multiple perspectives, and context that have become so important in modern life.

In contrast, in comprehending writing of an expository nature, the goal is to understand the author's argument and think about the significance of that argument. Langer (in press) characterizes expository reading as "maintaining a point of reference" (p. 37)—keeping in mind the point being made and getting closer and closer to the deeper significance of that position as one reads and thinks about what has been read.

Both kinds of reading should be emphasized in schools; indeed, both kinds should be integrated in the study of literary and expository works. To use an example from high school, *Pride and Prejudice* can be the basis for expository instruction examining Jane Austen's caution about the necessity for people to learn how to look beneath the surface attractiveness of people (the first suitor), to discern true quality (the second suitor), and the implications of that idea for how we live our lives (the message). Or the novel can be read for the literary engagement and self-searching that this story of a 19th-century heroine can bring to a 20th-century student (personal response).

Conversely, narrative is a powerful tool in teaching history or science; some of the best instruction asks students to argue from multiple perspectives. Commentators have accurately stressed that students are notoriously weak in the discursive—getting the point and evaluating and applying it—but unfortunately, most of our youngsters hardly ever experience nontrivial literary engagement with literature and nonfiction writing. One of the most welcome changes in some of the new reading program materials is the addition of a balance between literary and expository works. In addition, in the past several years there has been an explosion in the children's book market of informational titles in science, biography, history, and ethics.

In summary, according to Langer, Applebee, and other commentators, growing evidence supports the importance of exposure to expository reading materials and writing in expository modes. Langer and Applebee warn of the twin dangers of literary instruction degenerating into countenancing the most superficial personal reactions or expository instruction becoming sterile and trivial (Langer, in press). Some reform literature tends to downplay the significance of what

Applebee (1992a, 1992b, 1994) terms the author's "message" (emphasizing the moral lesson). Proper instruction depends on balancing three literary traditions—message, reader reaction and response, and textual analysis. All of these work together to deepen understanding (Applebee, 1991).

Unfortunately, much ELA instruction in elementary school neglects these strategies and settles for trivial recall questions, unmediated personal responses, and low-level follow-up activities. Many reformers warn against the mindless use of many activities that occupy the time of so many elementary students. For example, Lucy Calkins, highly respected in the ELA community, asks how doing a diorama (a craft display of an event in the book) helps develop deeper understanding. In addition, many schools and texts have underemphasized learning to understand expository text.

How to Produce More Meaningful Discussions

Discussions that delve into the deeper meanings of literary books and nonfiction should start early. Analytic comments and questions by the teacher have been shown to be major ingredients of success in effective preschool and kindergarten classes.

Leading productive discussions is a difficult art: Teachers need training both in understanding the potential issues in books children read and in the techniques of how to conduct a discussion. Several interesting projects have emerged during the past few years in the process of trying to encourage deeper classroom discussions and avoiding the trivial recall or "what happened" questions that pass for comprehension discussion in most schools. Although there are differences in philosophy and the approaches fall on different parts of the child-centered/text-centered continuum, all these projects share a common strategy of deepening the response to books and engaging children in conversations about what they read.

Lucy Calkins of Teachers College at Columbia University has instituted a book club program in New York that has small groups of students discuss books in groups. She also has pioneered individual conferencing with students to get them deeper into a book. Richard Anderson's (1995) "Learning to Argue" strategy[2] is aimed at the discourse side of literature. Students read a story about an immigrant Chinese American boy and discuss whether or not the boy's desire to change his name is a good thing or a bad thing to do. They learn to marshal arguments and justify positions. Taffy Raphael and Susan McMahon have instituted a successful book club program with local schools in Michigan (Raphael, 1994; see also Goatley, Brock, & Raphael, 1995; Raphael & Goatley, 1994; Raphael, Goatley, McMahon, & Woodman, 1995).[3] Isabelle Beck and Margaret McKeown have developed a "questioning the author" strategy that helps students take an active stance vis-à-vis the materials read (Beck, McKeown, Worthy, Sandora, & Kuean, 1993). The Reading for Real Program (ages 4 to 8) from Eric Schaps' Developmental Studies Center in Oakland, California, takes favorites of children's literature and helps teachers think about the possibilities for discussion. Junior Great Books of Chicago has a new series out for kindergarten and first grade. St. John's College in Annapolis, Maryland, has produced the Touchstones Discussion Project. Several of the best writing projects around the nation have now become involved in combining writing processes around deeper issues in literature and public discourse. Bob Calfee from Stanford University's Project READ has stressed critical literacy (Calfee & Patrick, 1995). Finally, Harvey Daniels (1994) from National Louis-University Center for City Schools in Chicago has developed a program for literature circles. Many of these projects use reading logs or follow-up activities as strategies.

Assessment

Until recently, ELA assessment has relied heavily on standardized reading tests based on national norms. In some instances, other formats such as the "cloze technique" (fill in the blank with a word) tests used by Degrees of Reading Power in New York have been utilized in large-scale assessment. Now, the New Standards Project and many other state efforts are compiling content standards, performance standards, scoring rubrics, and an assessment system of both multiple choice and performance tasks and student work. They have addressed the questions of how to assess many of the areas discussed in this book.

If standards-setting efforts such as these become the driving force in accountability, then a new mix of assessment devices must be developed. Some parts of any assessment system can still use multiple choice formats (e.g., for testing levels of comprehension or for efficient skills diagnosis). Some parts will need to chronicle the completion of important tasks, such as the number of books read or how fluent the child is, both of which must be assessed individually at the local school. Still others will need to assess student application of knowledge through larger tasks measured against scoring rubrics that represent a scale from high to low. For example, a scoring rubric can assess a student's ability to organize information, make an argument, or tell a story.

In addition, as discussed earlier, teachers and schools need to keep track of progress in reading (or writing, speaking, and listening) by using such devices as running records or miscue analysis. Finally, all teachers should learn to become adept "kid watchers" and develop strategies such as listening to oral reading to ascertain a student's strengths and weaknesses in order to plan appropriate instruction.

Benchmarks

States, districts, or schools should also adopt benchmark reading standards for each grade, as follows:

1. At the end of kindergarten, almost all children should know most letter names and shapes, some sounds, and possess defined levels of basic phonemic, print, and syntactic awareness.
2. By the middle of first grade, almost every child should know a significant number of letter/sound correspondences decoding and word-attack skills; reach designated levels of phonemic and syntactic awareness; be fluent with a specified number of sight words and families; and know how to spell a specified number of words. At this stage, the student should be able to read from actual books, decode, and self-correct.
3. By the end of first grade, children should be able to read a grade-level book with 95% accuracy and appropriate speed and inflection, and understand what was read. They should have read at least 100 little books or stories. They should reach specified levels of knowledge with more complex letter/sound correspondences, spelling, syllabication, vocabulary, and writing grammar and mechanics.
4. For subsequent grades, children should meet appropriate standards for that grade in the given strands, that is, read 25 to 35 fiction and informational books at grade level from acceptable lists. Students should also reach specified levels of performance appropriate to their grade in the additional standards of word

roots and affixes and the more complex skills such as syllabication, spelling, mechanics, grammar, and so on.

Notes

1. Arthur Applebee and Judith Langer are director and codirector, respectively, of the National Research Center on Literature Teaching and Learning,
University of New York at Albany, 1400 Washington Ave., Albany, New York
12222, Tel: (518) 442-5209.

2. Available from Richard C. Anderson, Director, Center for the Study of
Reading, University of Illinois, Urbana-Champaign, Champaign, Illinois
61820-5711, Tel: (217) 244-4501.

3. Taffy Raphael and her colleagues can be contacted at 304 Erickson
Hall, Michigan State University, East Lansing, Michigan 48824, Tel: (517)
355-1786.

8

Writing and Speaking

Written and Oral Applications

Students should be proficient in the major types of writing and oral presentation that occur in school and in the real world. Writing and speaking are usually divided into two broad categories—narrative (stories and storytelling) and expository (informing and persuading). Using the categories developed by the writing and English/Language Arts (ELA) community, students should be able to do the following:

- Organize material and present a written or oral report
- Tell a story or describe an event or setting
- Discuss a piece of literature or nonfiction
- Make an argument
- Recommend a course of action
- Convey information
- Participate in discussions

These writing and oral activities should be included as part of instruction throughout elementary school years. Performance should be consistent with standards established for each grade.

Writing

Some of the best writing curricula incorporating these guidelines have been devised by teachers in various writing projects around the country. Many of these projects have been in existence for several years and have helped thousands of teachers learn how to write and how to teach the process of writing. One of the central principles of this movement is that understanding is created by writing. They argue that until students write about something, their views are inchoate. Thus, keeping journals, free-writing techniques, multiple drafts, peer review, postponing editing until the final draft, and other techniques have emerged as ways to assist students to think through and organize their ideas before they write and then to rethink and revise their initial drafts. The aim of these techniques is to encourage students to think about what they are writing and in the process to refine, reformulate, and extend their understanding of a subject.

Although the process approach has now become the conventional wisdom among ELA professionals, some cautionary notes now are being raised about overreliance on this strategy. According to Arthur Applebee (1986, 1991, p. 401), who has also been one of the most respected commentators on the course of writing instruction in the past decade, the process approach arose as a response to the perceived ineffectiveness of the traditional composition classes in high school. Composition classes tended to emphasize correct usage and mechanics, the use of topic sentences, and formulas for paragraph construction. This instruction relied on sampling traditional modes of discourse and analyzing classic examples of good form in different discourses, such as narration or exposition; learning the rules that govern those examples; and practicing following those rules.

The process approach grew out of research showing that writing, rather than being a linear process, involves a number of "recursively operating subprocesses (for example, planning, monitoring, drafting, revision, editing)" (Applebee, 1986, p. 96), and that expert and novice writers differ in their use of those subprocesses. Thus, teach the processes.

One major problem with this strategy is that another important finding of what constitutes good writing—tailoring the use of processes to the nature of the task—was ignored. Much writing instruction in the process approach has become formulaic: It encourages students to go through the techniques, regardless of the nature of the task and detached from writing for a real purpose. The processes have become the end instead of the means.

According to Applebee (1986, p. 98 et seq.), 50% of all writing in high school occurs outside of the English class—much of it for review and reinforcement, not extension or refinement. Assignments outside of English classes are typically a page or less, first and final drafts are completed within a day, and the assignments serve to examine students in a subject matter. The personal and imaginative writing that dominates English instruction unfortunately has little place in these non-English classrooms. Process writing is overkill in these situations.

Thus there is a disjuncture between writing instruction in English classes and the writing occurring outside those classes. Obviously, part of the problem is that not enough activities requiring reasoning and problem solving are being assigned. But a major deficiency in writing instruction is that the strategic purpose for writing has been misconceptualized by too many.

Applebee (1986) posits three major purposes of writing. These are to

1. draw on relevant experience and knowledge in preparation for new activities,
2. consolidate and review new information and experiences, and
3. reformulate and extend knowledge.

Process writing instruction should be about figuring out which processes apply in which situation. Creative writing, which has become the mainstay of many elementary writing programs, applies only to a portion of the third purpose.

Another major problem with overreliance on a process approach is that content tends to become trivialized. The *how* of writing is not enough. *What* students think and write about is key to developing literacy skills. Some of the better writing projects, such as Carol Jago's California Literature Project at UCLA in partnership with Sheridan Blau's Santa Barbara Writing Project, now combine process learning with deep understanding of literature.

Finally, in reaction to student deficiencies in these areas, many writing projects are now attempting to put more emphasis on the correctness of the final product by insisting on proper spelling, punctuation, grammar, and mechanics, without losing the benefits of students putting their ideas on paper. Still other projects also are putting more emphasis on expository writing and public discourse to remedy the overreliance on narrative and expressive writing.

Speaking and Listening Skills

Rich discussions of text and student writing help children learn how to participate in sophisticated conversations. ELA curricula also should include some teaching of how to speak before the class, present a paper or piece of work, or conduct a briefing, and numerous opportunities to both present work and discuss other students' presentations. All grades should include listening to and discussing stories and other text. In preschool and kindergarten, there should be storytelling and retelling activities and listening to and repeating nursery rhymes and songs. Explanations should be added in early first grade and beginning group discussion by middle first grade. From second to fifth grades, students should be able to take turns and respond to what was said in group, be able to participate in class discussions and plays, and be able to recite.

Application of Speaking and Listening Skills

Much of math, history, and science instruction should also help develop these ELA skills. Classrooms should be rich with projects and assignments giving students opportunities to write and discuss materials. As mentioned earlier, the more there is discussion about books, ideas, and important matters, the more significant increases there are in listening comprehension, which affects reading comprehension (Juel, 1994, p. 126).

9

Frequently Asked Questions

How much time should be allocated to English/Language Arts (ELA) and which strands should be included?

Schools vary considerably in time allocations for reading. However, if schools are to reach the ambitious literacy goals outlined in this book, then a substantial amount of time must be devoted in primary grades to an integrated language arts program that includes an effective beginning-reading program. Such a comprehensive program must provide time for the following essential elements:

- Skills lessons
- Follow-up reading based on skill lessons
- Independent reading
- Word work
- Teaching writing and having students write
- Reading to and discussing literature and nonfiction with the students or having the students read multiple copies of a work and discuss it in the class or in small book club or literature circles
- Student projects
- Cross-discipline language-arts work
- Conferencing with and assessing students and giving feedback

For example, Slavin's "Success for All" requires 90 minutes a day just for the reading portion of ELA activities plus reading in the other subject matters. Some of the newly developed reading programs also recommend 90 minutes for English/Language Arts (ELA) instruction and many schools are devoting 2 to 3 hours. Anything less is probably not enough, since so many strands must be included in ELA time.

How much homework should be given?

In general, encouraging the right kind of additional work at home can substantially increase the effectiveness of any school program. Having parents read to children, discuss events, and encourage intellectual curiosity are activities obviously beneficial for beginning readers. Giving students the materials they read for their lessons to read again at home also is helpful. Most importantly, the bulk of independent reading should be done outside of school, and students should develop the habit of reading 15 to 30 minutes a night. Finally, specific writing assignments, school projects, or practicing skills constitute appropriate kinds of work at home.

How should bilingual students learn to read?

The same strategies outlined for English-speaking students also work well for Spanish-speaking students who are in bilingual programs because Spanish language is so regular. (Many non-English-speaking students will be taught in an English as a Second Language [ESL] program that teaches these students to read in English. ESL programs should also follow the strategies outlined in this book.) A bilingual strategy teaches students to read in their primary language under the theory that it is too difficult and confusing for a child to be learning a written and spoken second language and at the same time be trying to learn how to read. Once students become fluent readers in their primary language in the second to fourth grades, they then are taught to read in English so that they are reading on grade level in English by fifth grade.

Schools should adopt the same goals and instructional components outlined in this book for bilingual classes as for English-reading classes. Students should be fluent by the third grade in their primary language and be on grade level in English by the fifth grade.

In Asian bilingual classes the strategy is more problematic. Although these languages do use some character or phoneme pattern correspondences (Share, 1995, pp. 197-198), most are not based on the alphabetic principle. To read most Asian languages, early primary students must memorize large numbers of individual characters, word segments (radicals), or words. There is a fundamental question as to how much time and effort for memorization of these characters contributes to learning English. In Spanish, the same reading principles apply as in English, so that learning the system in Spanish will help students understand what reading English is about; this may not hold true for many Asian languages.

Can learning formal phonics rules help students learn to read?

Some people think phonics can be taught by spending considerable time on learning formal phonics rules on pronunciation of vowels (e.g., "In many two- and three-syllable words, the final *e* makes the preceding vowel long"), pronunciation of consonants, division of syllables, and accentuation of syllables. Not so, says Adams (1990, p. 272). First, it would take an enormous effort to memorize the approximately 121 rules. Moreover, in examining the most common 45 generalizations, researchers found an extremely low reliability rate, whereas the ones that did conform to the rules reliably were used infrequently. Many of the common ones were riddled with exceptions. For example, the rule cited above about lengthening vowels turns out to be true only 46% of the time.

Many generalizations use technical terms, such as *consonant* and *short vowel,* that are not really understood by many young children.

Another problem with learning to read by learning the rules is that most people find trying to apply an abstract rule to an immediate situation to be a very inefficient way of operating. Rules have to be consciously applied and can never substitute for speed of direct familiarity with the patterns to which they apply. (Think of trying to apply the grammar rules learned in taking a foreign language or even stopping to translate thoughts from English to Spanish in trying to speak or understand that language. The process must become unconscious and automatic to be effective.) Adams (1990) warns that "for neither the expert nor the novice can rote knowledge of an abstract rule, in and of itself, make any difference" (p. 272). Nevertheless,

Adams suggests that the use of some phonics rules is helpful in learning the patterns. Their use must be supplemental and resorted to only after the recognition system fails. They are helpful in getting students to attend to the pattern relationships in a word and can be used to overcome particular stumbling blocks with dyslexic children.

How do you get students back on track in later grades?

Schools must be able to determine where students are on phonemic awareness, decoding, word-attack, strategic-reading, comprehension, and spelling scales, and organize an effective support program. If a child does not know decoding skills, he or she must be taught. The same principles delineated in this book apply, although some of the sequences might be altered to respond to individual needs.

The best Title I and special education programs, clinics and individual tutors who deal with reading problems and dyslexia, and successful classrooms all can teach students to read and get them on the reading track, even if they are significantly behind. They must build on what these students know by improving their phonemic awareness, teaching them the symbol/sound relationships, and using high-interest reading material with more regular spellings. Of course, it will be difficult to make up for the texts they did not read when they were struggling. Schools need to focus resources to ensure that students learn these essentials.[1]

One interesting new development is the use of student-controlled tapes to support the reading process. Michael Shany and Andrew Biemiller (1995) significantly increased the reading comprehension of third and fourth graders who were poor readers by increasing the actual amount of time the students practiced reading. Students were able to speed up or slow down a tape of a story to try to match their own reading speed.

Can computers help teach reading?

Computer technology has advanced significantly in recent years and is now able to integrate manipulation of letters and sound. Speech recognition capability is just becoming feasible. Thus, computers can offer students who are learning to read or having trouble learning to read the large amount of practice and symbol/sound manipulation needed to develop phonemic sensitivity to the sound structure of words. These programs can also reinforce or teach word-identification skills and increase understanding of spelling patterns in words.[2] Dyslexic students, who need much more practice than other students to learn a particular skill, may especially benefit from computer-assisted learning.

As discussed above, much of the difficulty poor and dyslexic readers have in decoding words stems from poor phonological processing ability. This difficulty prevents them from developing an awareness of the phonological structure of words and the relationship between written and spoken language. As a result, much of beginning-reading instruction is incomprehensible to them (Torgesen & Barker, in press).

Torgesen and Barker (in press) have developed interactive, game-like phonological training programs for the computer called *Daisy-Quest* and *CastleQuest*. These programs for 4- to 7-year-olds include phonemic analysis (the ability to segment phonemes in whole words, phonemic synthesis (the ability to blend isolated phonemes together to produce words), phonemic identification (the ability to notice sound and rhyming similarities among words), and the ability to count, pronounce, or match phonemes with the letters in a word. These programs cannot yet provide the full set of activities because computer voice identification capabilities are not yet fully developed.

The program includes seven tasks: recognizing rhyming words, matching words on the basis of similar first sounds; matching on the basis of last sounds; matching on the basis of middle sounds; recognizing words presented in an onset/rime format (*s-ing, r-ing, th-ing*); making words out of individual phonemes; and counting the number of sounds in words. The programs have produced large improvements in reading comparable to those achieved by teacher tutors in the same activities.

Torgesen and Barker (in press) then conducted a study of first-grade students who were lagging behind their peers. A third of the students received 8 hours of training with *DaisyQuest* and *CastleQuest*. Another third received an equivalent amount of time in computer practice in learning to decode the middle vowels in short words. The final third—a treatment comparison group—spent the time practicing math on the computer.

The first group—those who received the phonemic awareness tasks on the computer—made significant gains in phonemic awareness, decoding, and reading skills compared to the other groups. Torgesen and Barker's next step is to develop computer activities that make the transition from phonological awareness as an oral language skill to utilizing phonological skills in reading and spelling. As stated earlier, the combination of phonemic awareness training and letter/sound training reinforces both (Torgesen & Barker, in press).

Torgesen also reviewed computer programs, including Isabelle Beck's 1984 *Hint and Hunt* and *Construct-a-Word,* which help children decode middle vowels and common word endings. Twenty hours of instruction with these programs produced a 2- to 4-year boost in reading (Torgesen & Barker, in press).

Additional computer-assisted reading programs that incorporate many of these ideas are under development in a variety of places for both school and home use. Richard Olson and Barbara Wise at the University of Colorado have been experimenting with different ways of communicating speech using synthetic speech. They are developing programs that allow students to select any word or word part on a screen for pronunciation. Students can hear the whole word, the syllables, or the onset-rime (*b-ack, s-ack*). The most learning disabled students were helped the greatest by the syllable feedback, the more advance readers by onset-rime (Torgesen & Barker, in press). This group is now researching which kind of feedback is most helpful to students with phonological processing problems while they are reading text.

Finally, computers offer a tremendous potential to assist teachers in assessment and diagnosis—keeping track of how students are learning particular skills, such as how many words or word families they can recognize, or which words they can spell correctly.

Similarly, the Waterford Institute's *Rusty and Rosy's Read With Me* program allows students to pick words and hear their pronunciation and construct words from onsets, and beginning, middle, and ending segments and hear the pronunciation of each segment. The Institute (in Sandy, Utah) has developed and released a preschool and kindergarten beginning-to-read computer program titled *Early Reading Program,* which has obtained significant improvement in diverse classroom settings. First- and second-grade versions are to follow soon. The Learning Company has released *Reader Rabbit's Journey* and *Read, Write, and Type,* and Scholastic has produced *Wiggleworks.* Finally, *SoundProof* won the Johns Hopkins National Search for Computing to Assist Persons With Disabilities Award, and the

Lindamood-Bell organization is working on a series of sophisticated computer segmentation and phonics tasks. Manipulating sounds and letters promises to offer cost-efficient ways of individualizing phonemic and phonic assistance and applying these tools to reading tasks.

Notes

1. For older students, see the *Journal of Reading: A Journal of Adolescent and Adult Literacy* from the International Reading Association in Newark, Delaware.

2. For a good review of this whole topic, see Torgesen and Barker (in press).

10

Conclusions
and Lessons Learned

If a primary goal of schooling is to help students become independent, lifelong learners, it is essential that they learn the skills and strategies to comprehend, interpret, and use increasingly complex written materials on their own. An extreme whole-language approach—which assumes learning to read develops only through exposure to literature and print without the assistance of a systematic program to teach the skills needed to unlock the language code—does not foster this independence for many children. Memorizing the large number of words used in technical and complex materials, as required by this method, is inefficient at best.

By learning to decode and recognize phonemic patterns and sound/symbol correspondences, students will possess the tools to decipher new words as they encounter them and become fluent with a growing number of words. A systematic learning-to-read program, together with a rich literature-based approach, will restore balance to the teaching of beginning reading and end this fruitless debate between the phonics and whole-language approaches. A truly "whole" reading program thoughtfully teaches skills and phonics and exuberantly awakens children to the richness of literature and the pursuit of meaning.

The Role of Skills in a Comprehensive Elementary Reading Program— 24 Major Points

The goal of any early reading program should be to enable almost every student to

- read fluently and understand grade-appropriate material by the end of elementary school;
- read a large number of books, magazines, and informational text;
- reach high levels of comprehension ability; and
- enjoy and be able to learn from reading.

This goal can be accomplished only if most students are reading beginning books by mid-first grade.

Why a Skills Strand Is an Essential Part of a Comprehensive Reading Program

All Children Need Skills Support

1. Language- and literature-rich classrooms are essential for effective reading programs, but almost all children need some organized skills instruction to reach optimal levels. For some groups of children, the consequences

of the absence of an explicit, organized skills strand are especially severe. Up to 40% of these students will remain, in effect, nonreaders, and significantly more than half will not read proficiently.

What Proficient Readers Do

2. Proficient readers recognize words automatically from their letter patterns aided by the meaning and context of what is being read.

How Students Become Fluent Readers

3. Proficient readers become automatic by recognizing a specific word *successfully* numerous times (in the range of 4 to 15 times during the early stages of reading). Encountering the word in the context of reading for meaning reduces the number of successful attempts necessary.

4. The most effective way for children to become fluent with a specific word is for them to consciously process both the letter patterns and sounds of the word the first few times it is read. For beginning readers, a combination of repeated reading of familiar material and tackling new material builds a critical mass of automatically recognized words, which in turn multiplies the number of books or materials a student can read.

Why Students Need to Successfully
Read Large Amounts of Material Early On

5. The pathway to reading fluency (recognizing 90% to 95% of the words for grade-appropriate material) is to read a substantial amount of text each year beginning at least by the middle of first grade. At the early grades, most stories or informational text will contain significant numbers of words important to the story that are already in the student's oral vocabulary but are not yet automatically recognizable in print. If students are to successfully read these materials, they must be able to decode new words.

Becoming Readers by Mid-First Grade

Establishing Goals

6. If a school, district, or state wants to maximize reading performance for all students, it should establish a goal that as many students as possible will become readers by mid-first grade. Only by achieving this measure of

independent reading of beginning materials will students encounter sufficient text early enough to become proficient. Only one out of eight students
who cannot read grade-appropriate materials at the end of first grade will
ever catch up without extraordinary tutoring strategies.

Benchmarks and Instruction: Kindergarten and Early First Grade

7. To become readers by mid-first grade, the following must occur:

- Students must leave *kindergarten* knowing letter names, shapes, and
  some letter sounds; possessing basic phonemic, syntactic, and print
  awareness; and having listening, discussion, and oral telling and
  retelling skills.
- During the first 4 months of first grade, they must learn basic
  sound/symbol system correspondences; more advanced phonemic
  and syntactic awareness; blending and word-attack strategic skills;
  automatic recognition of basic high-frequency words and word families; comprehension skills; and how to use these tools in combination
  to read for meaning. Writing out and spelling out words (especially
  those they are reading), which necessitates encoding sounds into
  letter patterns, is also one of the best ways to learn phonics.

The Relationship of Word Recognition, Decoding, and Phonemic Awareness

8. The most important component of reading ability in first grade is
word recognition, the most important component of word recognition is
decoding ability, and the most important components of decoding ability are
phonemic awareness (the ability to hear and consciously manipulate the
sounds in words) and phonics (knowing the system of letter/letter pattern/
sound correspondences and how to use that system in decoding words).

The Importance of Phonemic Awareness

9. An estimated one out of five children cannot learn decoding because
they cannot hear or consciously manipulate the sounds in words. Almost
every poor reader and more than 50% of special education youngsters lack
this proficiency in phonemic awareness; it cannot be overcome without
instruction.

10. Fortunately for the children who lack phonemic awareness, about 15 hours of specially designed kindergarten instruction (rhyming and word play), in addition to their regular instruction, will provide the necessary foundation to learn decoding in the first grade.

Instruction:
First Grade (January to June)

11. After the December or January milestone, students should read a large number (100 to 200) of beginning narrative and informational texts as the primary learning strategy to become automatic with increasing numbers of words. Teachers need to monitor progress.

Instruction:
Mid-First Grade On

Being Well-Read

12. Starting in late first grade, students should read about 25 to 35 age-appropriate fiction and informational books a year if they are to be grade-level readers by the end of elementary school. Students need to learn about 3,000 to 4,000 new vocabulary words (words not yet in their speaking vocabulary) each year during the elementary (and secondary) grades to be able to read and understand grade-appropriate material. Such a large number of words cannot be taught directly; most must be learned in the context of reading, although some words can be learned by listening to rich language.

Specific Comprehension Strategies

13. After initial basic comprehension instruction in how to read for meaning in first grade (supplemented by similar instruction about the stories read to or shown to children), an organized comprehension strand should be initiated that includes three components: independent reading, strategic reading, and book clubs or discussion of materials read in common utilizing a wide range of fiction and nonfiction materials to engender deep discussions about what has been read. All students should be able to read and understand a variety of grade-level materials as well as reach the higher comprehension levels of inferring, connecting, and applying what they have read.

Instruction in More Advanced Decoding, Complex Phonics,
Syllabication, Vocabulary, and Mechanics Skills

14. Skills instruction in more complex decoding strategies should continue after the beginning independent reading stage is reached in the more advanced areas of symbol/sound relationships, syllabication, spelling and mechanics, grammar, word roots and affixes, and vocabulary.

Writing

15. Students should have an organized writing program. Writing should prepare students to tell a story, organize a report, argue a point, and explain a phenomenon according to acceptable rubrics.

Temporary Spelling

16. Temporary or invented spellings (approximations) are appropriate in kindergarten and early first grade to help children write and to learn about the connection of sounds to letters. Invented spelling is also an extremely effective diagnostic tool to assist teachers in determining how well a student is learning phonics. However, starting in middle to later first grade, incorrect spellings should be corrected in final draft so that erroneous patterns are not reinforced.

Spelling

17. Students should have an organized spelling program from late first grade on. Learning to spell helps students learn to read. Spelling activities should be connected to the words students are reading and writing, systematically introduce them to orthographic patterns, and ensure that they learn spelling demons. Each week students should learn 7 to 10 words they cannot yet spell; these word lists should be tailored to each individual student. Instruction should incorporate the test-learning method to ensure students study only words they do not know, self-correcting of student tests, proofreading activities, and strategies for remembering spelling patterns. Students should practice using these words in writing.

Implications for Instruction

Flexibility

18. Most students will be able to meet the mid-first-grade timetable for independent reeading of beginning material. Some will reach this level

earlier. Some will take longer. Some will need intensified instruction (for example, more time with the teacher) to meet this timetable. Classrooms and schools should be able to accommodate these differences while bringing most children to this level by the mid-first-grade benchmark. When students can read beginning material independently, teachers must ensure that most of the material students read is in the 90% to 95% recognition range.

Dynamic, Not Rote Teaching

19. Phonemic awareness, phonics, and decoding should be taught in a dynamic, thinking manner so that students come to understand the alphabetic principle and the system of symbol/sound correspondences and how to consciously figure out new words. Programs should provide materials and activities that give students enough practice so that the particular skill being taught becomes second nature. Programs also should provide opportunities to develop and use these skills by having students read text with and without the teacher. A disconnected, worksheet-driven phonics program will not be effective.

Sufficient Time

20. In kindergarten, at least one third of the day should be devoted to language arts activities. In early primary grades, students should spend at least 2 to 3 hours in language arts activities, including reading and writing in the other subjects. At least 60 to 90 minutes of this time should be concentrated on reading and activities including guided, shared, and independent reading; student conferencing; the skills strands; and word play.

Availability of Reading Material

21. Reading material must be available so that students are continually reading at about the 95% recognition level (1 new word out of 20). If books are too easy, no growth occurs; if they are too hard, students become frustrated and will not become automatic with enough words. Teachers should ensure that books are appropriate to students' reading levels by continually conferencing with them. Students should read 100 to 200 "little" books or stories in first grade and 25 to 35 books after that. Narrative, informational, and magazine text should be available.

Role of Parents

22. Parents should be enlisted to support the development of their child's reading skills by reading to their child, listening to their child read, and discussing what has been read.

Intervention for Students
Who Are Falling Behind

23. If more intense instruction does not allow a student to meet reading milestones, tutors should be made available for those students not learning reading skills early. A back-up program of basic skills should be in place for students who transfer in at second grade or beyond or who need reinforcement.

Spanish-Speaking Children
in Bilingual Programs

24. Spanish-speaking students who are in bilingual classes should be able to reach the code-breaking or reading stage in their primary language a few months earlier (many of them by the end of kindergarten) than English speakers because Spanish is phonetically regular and has short syllable patterns. Bilingual programs should provide by the second to third grades a comprehensive and organized program for transition to English that reflects knowledge of the different pronunciation, syllable, and morphology (word roots and affixes) patterns between English and Spanish.

Reading Skills Curriculum Timeline—
Preschool Through Fifth Grade

The timeline in Table B-1 describes the specific skill development components of a reading program and when they should be taught. Each cell on the chart represents an essential component of literacy instruction. Instructional activities/**benchmarks** in each cell are representative of that component; they are not intended as a comprehensive list. (Benchmarks are printed in italics.)

Each area of the curriculum is reciprocally related (some more strongly than others)—for example, learning phonemic awareness helps learn letter/sound correspondence and vice versa. Children should be diagnosed regularly and intensified instruction or tutoring offered for those who fall behind. *All curricular areas up to January of first grade are aimed at enabling children in independently read beginning material.* This and other milestones in this chart are targets which *most* children should meet; of course, some will become independent readers earlier and some will take longer. Once independent reading is achieved, the goal is to keep students reading grade-appropriate text.

Table B-1

	Preschool	Kindergarten	First Grade: Fall*	First Grade: January to June*	Second Through Fifth
Listening and Discussion**	Listening to stories Discussing stories	Listening to stories Discussing stories	Listening to stories Discussing stories	Listening to stories Discussing stories	Listening to stories Discussing stories
Oral Discussion	Story telling Story re-telling Saying nursery rhymes	*Story telling* *Story re-telling* *Saying nursery rhymes*	Story telling Story re-telling Explanations	Story telling Explanations Beginning group discussions	Reports to class Group discussions —taking turns, responding Plays, recitations
Phonemic Awareness	Recognizing rhymes Hearing separate words Rhyming words	*Hearing syllables* *Rhyming words* *Oral comparisons* *Identification and blending of sounds* *Identifying syllables and word families* *Counting or matching the sounds of words*	*Segment initial, final, medial phonemes* *Blending phonemes* *Transpose cat to fat* *Deletion tasks*	*More complex segmentation, blending, and transpositions*	
Print Awareness	Pretend reading Recognizing signs	*Basic elements such as word boundaries, left to right sweeps*	*Full print awareness*		

(continued)

133

Table B-1 (Continued)

	Preschool	Kindergarten	First Grade: Fall*	First Grade: January to June*	Second through Fifth
Syntactic Awareness		*Understands how sentences and phrases work* *Understands word order* Shared reading	Anticipation of words Sentence structures Clues from mechanics —caps, periods, and commas	Beginning grammar Paragraphs	Text structure, e.g., story structure, poems, book reviews, newspaper articles, editorials More complex grammar
Letter Recognition	Exposure to letter names *Recognition of name*	*Knows most letter names* *Recognizes most letter shapes (upper and lower case)*	*Knows all letter names and shapes*		
Sound/Symbol Correspondence		*Knows some letter sounds*	*Knows basic letter and letter pattern/ sound correspondence*	*Complex letter/sound correspondences*	Remaining correspondences
Recognizing Word Families (words that sound alike and have similar letter patterns)		Attention to on-set and rimes, e.g., *r* and *ing* and *s* and *ing*	Recognizing basic word families patterns (37 rimes such as *in*, *or*, and *ill* make up 500 primary grade words)	Recognizing most of remaining 272 primary word families, e.g., *ine* and *ight*, which are regular	

Decoding/Word Attack			*Knows word-attack strategies: sounding out, comparing to similar words, breaking words into smaller words, looking for word parts, e.g., ing and ed, generating alternative pronunciations, using phonic, semantic, and syntactic clues, self-correction and self-monitoring* / *Guided reading*	Continued development of decoding ability, including use of more complex letter/sound correspondences, simple syllabication	Continued development of decoding ability, including use of complex letter/sound correspondences and word root/prefixes and suffixes
Recognizing High Frequency Words (irregular and regular)		*Knows some sight words*	*Automatically recognized 50 high-frequency words*	*Recognizes 150 high-frequency words*	

(continued)

Table B-1 (Continued)

	Preschool	Kindergarten	First Grade: Fall*	First Grade: January to June*	Second Through Fifth
Writing/Encoding	Pretend writing Making signs	Writes words (temporary spelling) Writes name Beginning story writing Group dictated stories	Beginning stages of writing stories, descriptions, persuasions, and reports. Beginning mechanics, e.g., punctuation and capitalization Beginning grammar and usage	Later stages of writing narratives, expository text such as organizing information for a report, arguing a point, etc. Continued mechanics, e.g., capitalization and punctuation More advanced grammar and usage	Writes competently: narratives, reports, advocacy, descriptions Can use mechanics: composition, e.g., sentence structure and paragraph structure; more adanced grammar and usage
Vocabulary—Meaning, Word Parts, Word Play	Word meanings from oral discussions and explanations	Word meanings from oral discussions and explanations Builds simple words with magnetic letters	Word meanings from oral discussions and explanations Learns some new words from reading Can use word derivations e.g., adding ed, ing, etc. Constructs words from given consonants and vowels, and patterns	Word meanings from oral discussions and explanations Some new words from reading Word structure Syllabication of simple words More complex word construction	Word meanings from oral discussions and explanations Most new words from reading—learning from context Syllabication of more complex words Knows system of word roots, suffixes, and prefixes Synonyms—best and creative word use Semantic trees

Spelling	Making signs	Temporary spelling	Temporary spelling Spells words in reading lessons	*Spells words in reading lessons* *Spells sound families and high-frequency words* *Spells individualized problem words* Corrects temporary spellings in final drafts	Individualized program based on words missed in writing, spelling demons, and spelling lists organized by sound theme Test-study-test Immediate self-correction of tests Proofreading Memory strategies
Independent Reading/ Assigned Reading/ Guided Reading	Reading good stories and nursery rhymes to children	Reading good stories and informational text to children	Reading for meaning of specifically designed books or appropriate material connected to lessons with teacher or partner Individual or group reading of simple text Reading good stories and informational text to children	Reading narrative and information text becomes the primary learning strategy *Reads and understands 100–200 "little books"* Teacher conferencing Students read and discuss stories, magazines, and informational text from anthologies, reading series, etc. Guided reading Teacher reads to children	*Reads and understands 25–35 grade-appropriate books each year from accepted fiction and nonfiction lists* Reads in depth Teacher conferencing Can engage in in-depth discussions Introduction to a variety of genres Reading in subject matter areas Guided reading Teacher reads to children

(continued)

Table B-1 (Continued)

	Preschool	Kindergarten	First Grade: Fall*	First Grade: January to June*	Second through Fifth
Specific Comprehension Strategies	Picture reading for meaning	Picture reading for meaning	Read for meaning	Read for meaning Discuss books *Can use beginning comprehension strategies—predicting, connecting to what is known, summarizing, etc.*	Discussions strategies, e.g., book clubs *Can use advanced strategic reading skills—predicting, summarizing, connecting, and visualizing*
Fluency			Re-reading of familiar material Oral reading	Re-reading of familiar material Expression Phrasing Oral reading	Continued work on expression, phrasing and oral reading *Can read orally— accurately, fluently and with expression*

NOTES: *For year-round or alternative year schedules, *Fall* means the first 4 months of first grade or equivalent, and *January to June* means the last 5½ months or equivalent.

**Italics indicate benchmarks for each grade level.

138

References

Adams, M. J. (1990). *Beginning to read: Thinking and learning about print.* Cambridge: MIT Press.

Adams, M. J. (1991). Why not phonics *and* whole language? In *All language and the creation of literacy* (pp. 40-53). Proceedings of the Orton Dyslexia Society Symposia, "Whole Language and Phonics" and "Literacy and Language." Baltimore, MD: Orton Dyslexia Society.

Adams, M. J., & Bruck, M. (1995). Resolving the "Great Debate." *American Educator, 19*(7), 10-20.

Anderson, R. C. (1992). *Research foundations for wide reading* (paper commissioned by the World Bank). Urbana, IL: Center for the Study of Reading.

Anderson, R. L., & Nagy, W. E. (1992). The vocabulary conundrum. *American Educator, 17,* 14-18, 44-49.

Anderson, R. C. (1995, April). *Children's argumentation during story discussions.* Invited address at the annual meeting of the American Educational Research Association, San Francisco.

Applebee, A. N. (1986). Problems in process approaches: Toward a reconceptualization of process instruction. In A. R. Petrosky & D. Bartholomae (Eds.). *The teaching of writing: Eighty-fifth year book of the National Society for the Study of Education* (pp. 95-113). Chicago: University of Chicago Press.

Applebee, A. N. (1991). Informal reasoning and writing instruction. In J. E. Voss, D. N. Perkins, & J. W. Segal (Eds.), *Informal reasoning and education* (pp. 401-414). Hillsdale, NJ: Lawrence Erlbaum.

Applebee, A. N. (1992a). The background for reform: Rethinking literature instruction. In J. A. Langer (Ed.), *Literature instruction: A focus on student response* (pp. 1-17). Urbana, IL: National Council of Teachers of English.

Applebee, A. N. (1992b). Stability and change in the high school canon. *English Journal, 81*(5), 27-32.

Applebee, A. N. (1994). Toward thoughtful curriculum: Fostering discipline-based conversation. *English Journal, 83*(2), 45-52.

Beck, I., & Juel, C. (1995). The role of decoding in learning to read. *American Educator, 19*(8), 21-25, 39-42.

Beck, I., McKeown, M., Worthy, J., Sandora, C., & Kuean, L. (1993). *Questioning the author: A year long classroom implementation to engage students with text.* Available from authors at the Learning Research Development Center, University of Pittsburgh.

Biemiller, A. (1994). Some observations on beginning reading instruction. *Educational Psychologist, 29,* 203-209.

Blachman, B. A. (1991). Getting ready to read: Learning how print maps to speech. In J. Kavanagh (Ed.), *The language continuum: From infancy to literacy* (pp. 1-22, reprint ed.). Washington, DC: U.S. Department of Health and Human Services.

Bowey, J. (1995). On the contribution of phonological sensitivity to phonological recoding. *Issues in Education, 1,* 65-69.

Brown, A. L., & Palincsar, A. S. (1984). Reciprocal teaching of comprehension fostering and comprehension monitoring. *Cognition and Instruction, 1,* 117-175.

Brown, R., Pressley, M., Schuder, T., & Van Meter, P. (1994). *A quasi-experimental validation of transactional strategies instruction with previously low-achieving grade-2 readers.* College Park: University of Maryland, National Reading Research Center.

Bryson, B. (1990). *The mother tongue: English & how it got that way.* New York: William Morrow.

Calfee, R. C. (1995). A behind-the-scenes look at reading acquisition. *Issues in Education, 1,* 77-82.

Calfee, R. C., & Patrick, C. L. (1995). *Teach our children well: Bringing K-12 education into the 21st century.* Stanford: Stanford Alumni Association.

California Department of Education. (1994). *I can learn: A handbook for parents, teachers, and students.* Sacramento: Author.

California Reading Task Force. (1995). *Every child a reader.* Sacramento: California Department of Education.

Carver, R. P., & Leibert, R. (1995). The effect of reading library books at different levels of difficulty upon gain in reading ability. *Reading Research Quarterly, 30,* 26-50.

Center, Y., Wheldall, K., Freeman, L., Outhred, L., & McNaught, M. (1995). An evaluation of Reading Recovery. *Reading Research Quarterly, 30,* 240-260.

Chall, J. S. (1983). *Learning to read: The great debate.* New York: McGraw-Hill.

Chall, J. S. (1989). Learning to read: The great debate 20 years later. *Phi Delta Kappan, 70,* 521-538.

Chall, J. S. (1992). The new reading debates: Evidence from science, art and ideology. *Teachers College Record, 94,* 315-328.

Chall, J. S. (1995). Ahead to the Greeks. *Issues in Education: Contributions From Educational Psychology, 1,* 83-85.

Claiborne, R. (1983). *Our marvelous native tongue: The life and times of the English language.* New York: Times Books.

Clay, M. M. (1991). *Becoming literate: The construction of inner control.* Portsmouth, NH: Heinemann.

Clay, M. M. (1993). *Reading Recovery: A guidebook for teachers in training.* Portsmouth, NH: Heinemann.

Clay, M. M. (1994). Introduction. In R. B. Ruddell et al. *Theoretical models of reading* (p. xii). Newark, DE: International Reading Association.

Crystal, D. (1995). *The Cambridge encyclopedia of the English language.* New York: Cambridge University Press.

Cunningham, A. (1990). Explicit versus implicit instruction in phonemic awareness. *Journal of Experimental Child Psychology, 50,* 429-444.

Cunningham, A., & Stanovich, K. E. (1993). Children's literacy environments and early word recognition subskills. *Reading and Writing: An Interdisciplinary Journal, 5,* 193-204.

Daniels, H. (1994). *Literature circles.* York, ME: Stenhouse.

Delpit, L. D. (1995). *Other people's children.* New York: New Press.

Depree, H., & Iversen S. (1994). *Early literacy in the classroom: A new standard for young readers.* Bothell, WA: The Wright Group.

Dickinson, D. K. (Ed.). (1994). *Bridges to literacy: Children, families, and schools.* Cambridge, MA: Blackwell.

Ehri, L. C. (1994). Development of the ability to read words. In R. Ruddell & H. Singer (Eds.), *Theoretical models and processes of reading* (4th ed.), (pp. 323-358). Newark, DE: International Reading Association.

Ehri, L. C. (in press). Phases of development in learning to read words by sight. *Journal of Research in Reading,* J. Oakhill, R. Beard, & D. Vincent.

Foorman, B. R. (in press). Research on "The great debate over whole-language approaches to reading instruction." *School Psychology Review.*

Goatley, V. J., Brock, C. H., & Raphael, T. E. (1995). Diverse learners participating in regular education "book clubs." *Reading Research Quarterly, 30*(3), 352-380.

Goldenberg, C. (1994). Promoting early literacy development among Spanish-speaking children: Lessons from two studies. In E. H. Heibert & B. M. Taylor (Eds.), *Getting reading right from the start: Effective early literacy intervention* (pp. 171-199). Boston: Allyn & Bacon.

Goodman, K. S. (1976). Reading: A psycholinguistic guessing game. In H. Singer & R. B. Ruddell (Eds.), *Theoretical models and processes of reading* (pp. 497-508). Newark, DE: International Reading Association.

Goodman, K. S. (1986). *What's whole in whole language?* Portsmouth, NH: Heinemann.

Goodman, K. S. (1992). Why whole language is today's agenda in education. *Language Arts, 69,* 354-363.

Graves, D. (1994). *A fresh look at writing.* Portsmouth, NH: Heinemann.

Griffith, P., & Olson, M. (1992). Phonemic awareness helps beginning readers break the code. *The Reading Teacher, 45,* 516-523.

Henry, M. C., Calfee, R., & La Salle, R. A. (1989). A structural approach to decoding and spelling. In S. McCormick & J. Zutell (Eds.), *Cognitive and social perspectives for literacy research and instruction: Thirty-eighth yearbook of the National Reading Conference* (pp. 155 et seq.). National Reading Conference.

Hiebert, E. H. (1994). Reading Recovery in the United States: What difference does it make to an age cohort? *Educational Researcher, 23*(9), 15-25.

Hiebert, E. H., & Taylor, B. M. (Eds.). (1994). *Getting reading right from the start: Effective early literacy intervention.* Boston: Allyn & Bacon.

Hoorn, J. V., Nourot, P. M., & Scales, B. (1993). *Play at the center of the curriculum.* New York: Macmillan.

Iversen, S., & Tunmer, W. E. (1993). Phonological processing skills and the Reading Recovery Program, *Journal of Educational Psychology, 85,* 112-120.

Johnson, T. D., & Louis, D. R. (1990). *Bringing it all together: A program for literacy.* Portsmouth, NH: Heinemann.

Juel, C. (1994). *Learning to read and write in one elementary school.* New York: Springer-Verlag.

Knapp, M. S., Shields, P. M., & Turnbull, B. J. (1995). Academic challenge in high poverty classrooms. *Phi Delta Kappan, 76,* 770-776.

Krashen, S. (1993). *The power of reading: Insights from the research.* Englewood, CO: Libraries Unlimited.

Langer, J. A. (1992) Rethinking literature instruction. In J. A. Langer (Ed.), *Literature instruction: A focus on student response* (pp. 35-53). Urbana, IL: National Council of Teachers of English.

Langer, J. A. (1993). Discussion as exploration: Literature and the horizon of possibilities. In G. E. Newell & R. K. Durst (Eds.), *Exploring texts: The role of discussion and writing in the teaching of literature* (pp. 23-43). Norwood, MA: Christopher-Gordon.

Langer, J. A. (1994). Focus on research: A response-based approach to reading literature. *Language Arts, 71,* 203-211.

Langer, J. A. (in press). Literature and learning to think. *Journal of Curriculum and Supervision.*

Liberman, I. Y., Shankweiler, D., & Liberman, A. M. (1991). The alphabetic principle and learning to read. In *Phonology and reading disability: Solving the reading puzzle.* Washington, DC: International Academy for Research in Learning Disabilities, Monograph Series, U.S. Department of Health and Human Services, Public Health Service; National Institutes of Health.

Lindamood, P. C., Bell, N., & Lindamood, P. (1992). Issues in phonological awareness assessment. *Annals of Dyslexia, 42,* 242-259.

Lundberg, L. (1991). Phonemic awareness can be developed without reading processes. In *Literacy: A tribute to Isabelle Y. Liberman* (pp. 47-53). Hillsdale, NJ: Lawrence Erlbaum.

Lyon, G. R. (1994). *Research in learning disabilities at the NICHD.* Bethesda, MD: NICHD Technical Document/Human Learning and Behavior Branch.

Lyon, G. R. (1995). Research initiatives in learning disabilities: Contributions from scientists supported by the National Institute of Child Health and Human Development. *Journal of Child Neurology, 10,* 120-128.

Lyons, C. A., & Beaver, J. (1995). Reducing retention and learning disability placement through Reading Recovery: An educationally sound cost-effective choice. In R. Allington & S. Walmsley (Eds.), *No quick fix: Rethinking literacy programs in America's elementary schools* (pp. 116-136). New York: Teachers College Press.

McKeown, M. G., & Curtis, M. E. (Eds.). (1987). *The nature of vocabulary acquisition.* Hillsdale, NJ: Lawrence Erlbaum.

McPike, E. (1995). Learning to read: Schooling's first mission. *American Educator, 19,* pp. 12-15.

Moats, L. C. (1994). The missing foundation in teacher education: Knowledge of the structure of spoken and written language. *Annals of Dyslexia, 44,* 157-168.

Moran, C., & Calfee, R. C. (1993). Comprehending orthography; Social construction of letter-sound in monolingual and bilingual programs. *Reading and Writing: An Interdisciplinary Journal, 5,* 205-225.

Nagy, W. E. (1988). *Teaching vocabulary to improve reading comprehension.* Newark, DE: International Reading Association.

Nagy, W. E. (1995, April). *What do we know about vocabulary? Toward a state-of-the-art.* Panel presentation and interactive symposium at the American Educational Research Association, San Francisco.

Pearson, D. P. (1993). Focus on research: Teaching and learning reading: A research perspective. *Language Arts, 70,* 502-511.

Pinker, S. (1994). *The language instinct: How the mind creates language.* New York: HarperPerennial.

Pinnell, G. S., DeFord, D. E., Lyons, C. A., & Bryk, A. (1995). Response to Rasinski. *Reading Research Quarterly, 30,* 272-275.

Pinnell, G. S., Lyons, C. A., DeFord, D. E., Bryk, A. S., & Seltzer, M. (1994). Comparing instructional models for the literacy education of high risk first graders. *Reading Research Quarterly, 29,* 8-39.

Pinnell, G. S., Pikulski, J. J., Wixson, K. K., Cambell, J. R., Gough, P. B., & Beatty, A. S. (1995). *Listening to children read aloud: Data from NAEP's Integrated Reading Performance Record (IRPR) at Grade 4.* Washington, DC: National Center for Education Statistics (NCES 95-726).

Pressley, M., & Cariglia-Bull, T. (1995). Decoding and the beginnings of reading. In M. Pressley & V. Woloshyn (Eds.), *Cognitive strategy instruction that really improves children's academic performance* (2nd ed., pp.19-56). Cambridge, MA: Brookline Books.

Pressley, M., El-Dinary, P. B., Gaskins, I., Schuder, T., Bergman, J. C., Almasi, J., & Brown, R. (1992). Beyond direct explanation: Transformational treatment of reading comprehension strategies. *Elementary School Journal, 92,* 513-556.

Pressley, M., & Lysynchuk, L. (1995). Vocabulary. In M. Pressley & V. Woloshyn (Eds.), *Cognitive strategy instruction that really improves children's academic performance* (2nd Ed., pp. 101-115). Cambridge, MA: Brookline Books.

Pressley, M., & Rankin, J. (1994). More about whole language methods of reading instruction for students at risk for early reading failure. *Learning Disabilities Research & Practice, 9,* 157-168.

Pressley, M., Symons, S., McGoldrick, J. A., & Snyder, B. L. (1995). Reading comprehension strategies. In M. Pressley & V. Woloshyn (Eds.), *Cognitive strategy instruction that really improves children's academic performance* (2nd ed., pp. 57-100). Cambridge, MA: Brookline Books.

Raphael, T. (1994) Book club: An alternative framework for reading instruction. *The Reading Teacher, 48,* 102-116.

Raphael, T., & Goatley, V. J. (1994). The teacher as "More Knowledgeable Other." National Reading Conference Yearbook, Proceedings, 1994.

Raphael, T., Goatley, V., McMahon, S., & Woodman, D. (1995). Teaching literacy through student book clubs: Promoting meaningful conversations about books. In N. Roser & M. Martinez (Eds.), *Supporting children's responses to literature: Book talk and beyond.* Newark, DE: International Reading Association.

Rasinski, T. (1995a). On the effects of Reading Recovery: A response to Pinnell, Lyons, DeFord, Bryk, & Seltzer. *Reading Research Quarterly, 30,* 264-270.

Rasinski, T. (1995b). Reply to Pinnell, DeFord, Lyons, & Bryk. *Reading Research Quarterly, 30,* 276-277.

Rosenshine, B., & Meister, C. (1994). Reciprocal teaching: A review of the research. *Review of Educational Research, 64,* 479-530.

Scott, J. A., Hiebert, E. H., & Anderson, R. C. (1994). Research as we approach the millenium: Beyond "Becoming a Nation of Readers." In F. Lehr & J. Osborn (Eds.), *Reading, language, and literacy: Instruction for the twenty-first century* (pp. 253-280). Hillsdale, NJ: Lawrence Erlbaum.

Shany, M. T., & Biemiller, A. (1995). Assisted reading practice: Effects on performance for poor readers in Grades 3 & 4. *Reading Research Quarterly, 50*(3), 382-395.

Share, D. L. (1995). Phonological recoding and self-teaching: Sine qua non of reading acquisition. *Cognition: International Journal of Cognitive Science, 55,* 151-218.

Share, D. L., & Stanovich, K. E. (1995a). Accommodating individual differences in critiques: Replies to our commentators. *Issues in Education: Contributions From Educational Psychology, 1,* 105-121.

Share, D. L., & Stanovich, K. E. (1995b). Cognitive processes in early reading development: Accommodating individual differences into a mode of acquisition. *Issues in Education: Contributions From Educational Psychology, 1,* 1-57.

Shefelbine, J. (1995). Learning and using phonics in beginning reading. *Scholastic Literacy Research Papers, 10.* New York: Scholastic.

Shu, H., Anderson, R., & Shang, H. (1995). Incidental learning of word meanings while reading. *Reading Research Quarterly, 30,* 76-86.

Slavin, R. E., Madden, M. A., Dolan, L. J., Wasik, B. A., Ross, S., & Smith, L. (1994). "Whenever and wherever we choose. . . ." The replication of "Success for All." *Phi Delta Kappan, 75,* 639-647.

Slavin, R. E., & Madden, N. (1995, April). *Effects of "Success for All" on the achievement of English language learners.* Paper presented at the annual meeting of the American Educational Research Association, San Francisco.

Slavin, R. E., Madden, N. A., Dolan, L. J., & Wasik, B. A. (1995, April). *"Success for All": A multi-site replicated experiment.* Paper presented at the annual meeting of the American Educational Research Association, San Francisco.

Smith, F. S. (1982). *Understanding reading* (3rd ed.). New York: Holt, Rinehart & Winston.

Smith, F. S. (1992). Learning to read: The never-ending debate. *Phi Delta Kappan, 73,* 432-441.

Stahl, S. A. (1992). Saying the "p" word: Nine guidelines for exemplary phonics instruction. *The Reading Teacher, 45,* 618-625.

Stanovich, K. E. (1986). Matthew effects in reading: Some consequences of individual differences in the acquisition of literacy. *Reading Research Quarterly, 21,* 360-407.

Stanovich, K. E. (1993). Does reading make you smarter? Literacy and the development of verbal intelligence. In H. Reese (Ed.), *Advances in child development and behavior* (Vol. 25, pp. 133-180). San Diego, CA: Academic Press.

Topping, K. J. (1995). Cued spelling: A powerful technique for parent and peer tutoring, *The Reading Teacher, 48,*(5).

Torgesen, J. K. (1995). Instruction for reading disabled children: Questions about knowledge into practice. *Issues in Education: Contributions From Educational Psychology, 1,* 91-95.

Torgesen, J. K., & Barker, T. A. (in press). Computers as aids in the prevention and remediation of reading disabilities. *Learning Disabilities Quarterly.*

Torgesen, J. K., & Hecht, S. A. (in press). Preventing and remediating reading disabilities: Instructional variables that make a difference for special students. In M. F. Graves, B. M. Taylor, & P. van den Broek (Eds.), *The first right of all children.* Cambridge: MIT Press.

Tunmer, W. E., & Chapman, J. W. (1995). Context use in early reading development: Premature exclusion of a source of individual differences? *Issues in Education: Contributions From Educational Psychology, 1,* 97-100.

Watts, S., & Graves, M. (1995). *Fostering word consciousness.* Unpublished manuscript.

Williams, J. P. (1991). The meaning of a phonics base for reading instruction. In *All language and the creation of literacy* (pp. 9-19). Proceedings of the Orton Dyslexia Society Symposia, "Whole Language and Phonics" and "Literacy and Language." Baltimore, MD: Orton Dyslexia Society.

Woloshyn, V., & Pressley, M. (1995). Spelling. In M. Pressley & V. Woloshyn (Eds.), *Cognitive strategy instruction that* really *improves children's academic performance* (2nd ed., pp. 116-152). Cambridge, MA: Brookline Books.

Yopp, H. K. (1992). Developing phonemic awareness in young children. *The Reading Teacher, 45,* 696-703.

Yopp, H. K. (1995). A test for assessing phonemic awareness in young children. *The Reading Teacher, 49,* 20-29.

Index

ABC books, 28
Adams, M. J., 2, 6-8, 16-25, 27-32, 34-37, 52, 55, 57, 60, 64, 66, 77, 84, 92-95, 98, 103, 118-119, 139
Alliteration, 32
Almasi, J., 144
Alphabetic phase, 48-49
Alphabetic principle, 30, 31
  English versus other languages, 47
  learning, 51
Alphabet Song, 26, 28, 37
Anderson, R. C., 101-103, 106, 108-109, 111, 139, 146
Applebee, A. N., 106, 107-108, 111, 113-114, 139-140
Asian language children, 118
Assessment, 109-111
  first-grade level, 52-54, 64-65, 85-88
  kindergarten level, 34
  phonemic awareness, 34, 52-54
  upper elementary grades, 85-88
Assigned reading, 39, 137
Automatic reading, 45-49, 60

Barker, T. A., 37, 52, 120-122, 147
Beaver, J., 80, 144
Beck, I., 109, 121, 140
Beginning-to-read instruction, 2, 8, 9
  early first grade, 39-82
  prereading, 46
  preschool and kindergarten, 25-38
  standards, 12
Beginning writing, 29, 50, 98-99
Bell, N., 54, 143
Benchmarks. See Reading benchmarks
Bergman, J. C., 144
Biemiller, A., 5, 19-20, 102, 119, 140, 145
Bilingual programs, 117-118, 131
Blachman, B. A., 33, 37, 54, 140
Blau, S., 114
Books:
  discussion, 26-27, 105-109, 112
  matching books to students' levels, 84-85
  used in reading curriculum, 66-67
Bowey, J., 34, 140
Brock, C. H., 142

Brown, A. L., 104, 105, 140
Brown, R., 144
Bryk, A. S., 81, 85, 144
Bryson, B., 90, 140

Calfee, R. C., 48, 55-56, 88, 100, 109, 140, 142, 144
California Department of Education, 7, 12, 140
California Reading Task Force, 140
Cariglia-Bull, T., 21, 22, 26-27, 63, 145
Carver, R. P., 86-87, 141
CastleQuest program, 120
Center, Y., 81, 141
Chall, J. S., 2-3, 48, 141
Chapman, J. W., 46, 147
Chinese language, logographic learning, 47
Cipher knowledge, 41, 44, 68-69, 98
Claiborne, R., 90, 141
Clay, M. M., 2, 29, 34-35, 63, 67, 74, 78, 79, 92, 141
Cloze technique, 109
Comprehension. See Reading comprehension
Computer technology, reading curriculum, 119-122
Consolidated alphabetic phase, 49
Construct-a-Word program, 121
Context processing, 18, 23, 42
Crystal, D., 90, 141
Cunningham, A., 29, 44, 52, 54, 141
Curtis, M. E., 100, 109, 144

DaisyQuest program, 120
Daniels, H., 141
Decoding, 21-22, 127
  alphabetic phase, 48-49
  automatic reading, 46
  benchmarks, 135
  disabled readers, 14
  first grade, 39-43, 50, 51, 87
  learning disabled students, 6, 13-15
  phonemic awareness and, 40, 41-43
  upper elementary grades, 87
  word-attack strategies, 60-62
  word recognition, 21-22, 40, 49

DeFord, D. E., 81, 85, 144
Delpit, L. D., 6, 141
Depree, H., 3, 141
Discussing books, 26-27, 105-109, 112
Dolan, L. J., 82, 146
Dyslexic students, 6, 14, 42, 119, 120

Early Literacy Inservice Course, 37
Ehri, L. C., 19, 45, 47-50, 141, 142
El-Dinary, P. B., 144
Encoding, 62, 91, 135
English language, 47, 55, 58-59, 88
ESL programs, 117

Farkas, G., 25, 71, 81
Fifth-grade reading instruction, 103. *See also*
     Upper elementary grade reading instruc-
     tion
First-grade reading instruction, 83-84, 89
     assessment, 52-54, 64-65, 85-88
     automatic reading, 45-49
     benchmarks, 10-11, 22, 64-65, 110, 126-
        127, 133-138
     books and materials, 66-68
     components, 50
     correctness versus coverage, 68-69
     curriculum timeline, 133-138
     decoding, 41-43, 87
     early months, 39-82
     grouping strategies, 77-78
     instruction, 51-64
     instructional materials, 66-68
     intervention programs, 69-71, 74-77
     letter/sound correspondence, 87
     matching books to student level, 84-85
     middle months, 83-90
     phonemic awareness, 32, 39, 40
     phonics, 42, 50, 67
     practicing skills with an adult, 65-66
     reading comprehension, 40, 44-45
     rereading, 63-64
     spelling, 87, 94
     successful programs, 71-74
     syllables, 87-88
     teaching strategies, 39-40, 50-51, 67-68,
        78-79, 83-84
     tutoring, 70-71
     word recognition, 41
     word roots, 87-88
     writing ability, 98
Fluency, 18-22, 50, 63, 126, 138
Foorman, B. R., 5, 60, 142
Fourth-grade reading instruction. *See* Upper
     elementary grade reading instruction
Frameworks program, 37
Freeman, L., 141

Gaskins, I., 144
Goatley, V. J., 109, 142, 145
Goldenberg, C., 38, 142
Goodman, K. S., 4, 142
Graphonemes, 55
Graves, D., 93, 142
Griffith, P., 33, 142
Grouping strategies, 77-78, 86
Group tutoring, 70-71
Guided reading, 84, 137

Head Start program, 35
Hearing impairment, reading skills and, 31
Hecht, S. A., 29, 147
Henry, M. C., 88, 100, 142
Hiebert, E. H., 71, 81, 142
High-frequency words, 62, 83-84, 135
Hint and Hunt program, 121
Home environment, literacy, 26-27, 130
Homework, 117
Hoorn, J. V., 36, 142

Independent reading, 39, 84, 137
Individualized reading programs, 104
Individual tutoring, 70-71
Integrated language arts program, 116-117
Intervention programs, first grade, 69-71,
     74-77
Invented spelling, 91-92
Iversen, S., 3, 78, 141, 143

Jago, C., 114
Johnson, T. D., 65, 82, 143
Juel, C., 2, 6, 17, 19, 29, 30, 34, 40-45, 47,
     64-70, 79-80, 81, 84, 86, 98, 99, 103,
     115, 143
Junior Great Books, 109

Kindergarten reading instruction, 25-38
     assessment, 34
     beginning writing, 29
     benchmarks, 10, 110, 133-138
     curriculum timeline, 133-138
     letter recognition and naming, 27-29
     phonemic awareness, 29-34
     prereading, 46
     print awareness, 34-35
     syntactic awareness, 35
Klein, F., 82
Knapp, M. S., 3-4, 143
Krashen, S., 103, 143
Kuean, L., 109, 140

Langer, J. A., 106-108, 111, 143
Language development, 13-14, 29-30, 31, 47
La Salle, R. A., 87, 100, 142
Learning disabled students, 6
Leibert, R., 86-87, 141
Letter naming. *See* Naming letters
Letter recognition, 27
    benchmarks, 134
    first grade, 52
    naming letters, 27-28
    skilled readers, 16-17
    statistics, 37
    teaching, 27-29
Letter/sound correspondence:
    first grade, 51, 53, 54-59, 87
    instruction, 54-59
    phonemic awareness, 51
    upper elementary grades, 87
Lexical knowledge, 41, 79
Lexical learning, 47
Liberman, A. M., 5, 30, 31, 50, 143
Liberman, I. Y., 5, 6, 29-31, 50, 143
Lindamood, P., 54, 143
Lindamood, P. C., 54, 143
Lindamood-Bell Learning Process, 33-34, 37
Listening comprehension, 41, 44, 50, 63
Listening skills, 115
Listening to stories, preschool and kinder-
    garten, 26-27
Literacy:
    home environment, 26-27
    myths regarding reading, 4-8
    performance standards, 12
    statistics, 5, 14, 25, 30, 31, 37, 68
    strategy, 9-11
    whole language techniques, 2-8
    See also Reading; Reading curriculum
Logographical learning, 47
Logographic phase, 46
Look-say method, 47-48
Louis, D. R., 65, 82, 143
Low socioeconomic group children, 5, 34-35,
    40-44, 98-99
Lundberg, L., 30, 143
Lyon, G. R., 6, 14-15, 40, 143
Lyons, C. A., 80, 81, 85, 144
Lysynchuk, L., 100, 103, 145

Madden, M. A., 82, 146
Magnetic letters, 28
Matthew effect, 44
McGoldrick, J. A., 105, 145
McKeown, M. G., 100, 109, 140, 144
McMahon, S., 109, 145
McNaught, M., 141
McPike, E., 2, 144
Meaning processing, 18, 23

Meister, C., 104, 145
Memorization, word recognition, 47, 61
Metaphonics program, 56
Moats, L. C., 6, 75, 144
Moran, C., 55, 88, 100, 144
Morpheme, 87

Nagy, W. E., 88, 100, 144
Naming letters, 27-29, 50
Nourot, P. M., 36, 142
Nursery rhymes, 32

Oddity tasks, 32
Odd-picture-out, 33
Olson, M., 33, 142
Olson, R., 121
Oral discussion, 26-27, 105-109, 112, 133
Oral fluency, 30
Oral reading, first grade, 50
Orthographic phase, 49
Orthographic processing, 18, 36, 94
Outhred, L., 141

Palincsar, A. S., 104, 140
Partial alphabetic phase, 46-48
Patrick, C. L., 109, 140
Pearson, D. P., 2, 3, 16-17, 21, 144
Phonemes, 55
Phonemic awareness, 22, 29-31, 127-128
    activities, 32-34, 120
    assessment, 34, 52-54
    balanced approach, 8
    benchmarks, 133
    cipher knowledge, 44, 98
    decoding and, 40, 41-43
    first grade, 40-43, 50, 51, 52-54
    kindergarten, 30-34
    letter/sound correspondence, 51
    low socioeconomic group children, 42-43
    phonics, 42, 43, 67
    teaching, 31-34, 39-40, 52-54
    writing, 98
Phonemic blending, 32, 53
Phonemic segmentation, 32, 33, 37, 42, 53
Phonics, 22
    automatic recognition, 48
    balanced approach, 8
    first grade, 42, 50, 67
    formal rules, 118-119
    learning disabled students, 6, 13-15
    myths about, 8
    phonemic awareness, 42, 43, 67
    remedial, 75
    Spanish-speaking children, 38
    word recognition, 20

Phonological processing, 18, 22, 23, 36
    disabled readers, 14, 120
    letter recognition, 28
Phonological recoding, 45, 46, 48
Phonologic awareness, dyslexic students, 42
Pikulski, J. J., 6, 20, 144
Pinker, S., 14, 30, 144
Pinnell, G. S., 6, 20, 81, 82, 85, 90, 144
Play activities, as precursors to reading, 36
Pre-alphabetic phase, 47
Prereading, 46
Preschool reading instruction, 25-38
    beginning writing, 29
    benchmarks, 133-138
    curriculum timeline, 133-138
    learning-to-read sequence, 40-41
    letter recognition and naming, 27-29
    phonemic awareness, 29-34
    print awareness, 34-35
    syntactic awareness, 35
    word recognition, 41
Pressley, M., 2, 4, 7-9, 12, 21-22, 26-27, 31,
        63, 67, 74, 79, 93-97, 103, 105, 140,
        145, 147
Print awareness:
    benchmarks, 133
    first grade, 42, 50, 52
    kindergarten, 34-35
    lexical knowledge, 79
    low socioeconomic children, 34-35
Proficiency. See Reading proficiency

Rankin, J., 2, 4, 7-9, 12, 31, 67, 74, 79, 105,
        145
Raphael, T. E., 109, 111, 142, 145
Rasinski, T., 81, 145
Reading:
    automatic reading, 45-49, 60
    frequently asked questions, 116-122
    high poverty areas, 5-6
    learning disabled students, 6
    low socioeconomic children, 5, 34-35, 40-
        44
    matching books to students' levels, 84-85
    myths, 4-8
    performance standards, 12
    practicing skills with an adult, 65-66
    precursors in play, 36
    strategic reading, 104-105
    See also Reading benchmarks; Reading
        comprehension; Reading curriculum;
        Reading proficiency
Reading benchmarks, 133-138
    fifth grade, 103
    first grade, 10-11, 22, 64-65, 110, 126-127
    kindergarten, 10, 110
    upper grades, 103, 110-111

Reading comprehension, 44-45, 101-109
    benchmarks, 137
    discussion of books, 105-109
    first-grade level, 40
    listening comprehension, 41
    reading a lot, 102-103
    strategic reading, 104-105
    strategies, 105, 128
    vocabulary, 102
    word recognition, 40
Reading curriculum, 8-9, 12-13, 121
    assessment, 109-111
    balanced approach, 11-12, 37-38
    benchmarks, 133-138
    bilingual programs, 117-118
    comprehensive program, 125-131
    computer technology, 119-122
    curriculum timeline, 132-138
    frequently asked questions, 116-122
    homework, 117
    individualized reading programs, 104
    integrated language arts program, 116-117
    intervention programs, 69-71, 74-77, 119,
        131
    skills-based instruction, 2, 4, 5, 13, 14
    theory, 2-8
    See also First-grade reading instruction;
        Kindergarten reading instruction; Pre-
        school reading instruction; Reading
        benchmarks; Reading comprehension;
        Teaching strategies; Upper elementary
        grade reading instruction
Reading disability, 14-15, 21
Reading proficiency, 5, 18-22, 51, 126
Reading for Real program, 109
"Reading Recovery" program, 70, 71, 74-79,
        80-82, 85, 105
Reciprocal Teaching, 104
Recoding, 23, 45, 46, 48
Recognizing letters. See Letter recognition
Rereading, 63-64
Rhymes, 32
"Roots and Wings" program, 74
Rosenshine, B., 104, 145
Rusty and Rosy's Read With Me program, 121

Sandora, C., 109, 140
Say-it-and-move-it, 33
Scales, B., 36, 142
Schuder, T., 105, 140, 144
Second-grade reading instruction, 41, 94. See
        also Upper elementary grade reading
        instruction
Segmentation. See Phonemic segmentation
Self-teaching model, 45, 52
Seltzer, M., 81, 85, 144
Shang, H., 102, 146

Shankweiler, D., 5, 31, 50, 143
Shany, M. T., 102, 119, 145
Share, D. L., 2, 4-5, 17, 19-22, 24, 29, 31-32, 45-48, 53, 61, 80, 146
Shields, P. M., 3-4, 143
Shu, H., 102, 146
Slavin, R. E., 36, 71, 73-75, 81-82, 117, 146
Sligerland technique, 54
Smith, F. S., 4, 146
Snyder, B. L., 105, 145
Sounding out, 60-61
SoundProof program, 121
Sound/symbol correspondence. *See* Letter/sound correspondence
Spanish-speaking children, 37, 38, 118, 131
Speaking skills, 115
Special education students, 5-6
Speech development, 29-30
Spelling, 91, 91-98, 129
    as reading instruction tool, 62
    benchmarks, 136
    cipher knowledge, 98
    first-grade reading instruction, 87
    importance, 93
    invented spelling, 91-92
    teaching strategies, 95-98
    temporary spelling, 91-92, 129
Stahl, S., 2, 146
Stanovich, K. E., 2, 4-5, 17, 19-22, 24, 29, 31, 44-48, 75, 80, 102, 141, 146
Strategic reading, 104-105
"Success for All" program, 36, 71, 73-75, 77, 81, 105, 117
Summarization, 105
Syllables, 87-88, 129
Symons, S., 105, 145
Syntactic awareness, 35, 42, 50, 63, 134

Taylor, B., 71, 142
Teaching strategies:
    Asian bilingual students, 118
    bilingual programs, 117-118, 131
    first grade, 39-40, 50-51, 67-68, 78-79, 83-84
    letter recognition, 27-29
    oral discussion, 108-109
    phonemic awareness, 31-34, 39-40, 52-54
    preschool and kindergarten, 27-35
    reading comprehension, 105, 128
    Spanish-speaking children, 37, 38, 118, 131
    spelling, 95-98
    vocabulary, 100
    worksheet assignments, 67-68, 75, 89
Temporary spelling, 91-92, 129
Third-grade reading instruction. *See* Upper elementary grade reading instruction
Topping, K. J., 93, 146
Torgesen, J. K., 29, 37, 52, 120-122, 147

Tunmer, W. E., 3, 46, 78, 141, 143, 147
Turnbull, B. J., 3-4, 143
Tutoring, 70-71

Upper elementary grade reading instruction, 83-90
    assessment, 85-87
    benchmarks, 103, 110-111, 133-138
    curriculum timeline, 133-138
    decoding, 87
    letter/sound correspondence, 87
    matching books to student level, 84-85
    oral discussion, 105-109
    reading comprehension, 105
    skills development, 88-89
    syllables, 87-88
    word roots, 87-88

Van Meter, P., 105, 140
Visual processing, 23
Vocabulary, 99-100, 129
    benchmarks, 136
    fifth grade, 103
    first grade, 63
    reading comprehension, 102

Wasik, B. A., 82, 146
Wheldall, K., 141
Whole-language techniques, 2-8, 13, 30-31
Williams, J. P., 2, 147
Wise, B., 121
Woloshyn, V., 93, 94, 95-97, 147
Woodman, D., 109, 145
Word-attack strategies, 60-62
Word families, 34, 49, 60
Word play, 55-56
Word recognition, 16-20, 41, 127
    alphabetic principle, 47
    benchmarks, 134, 135
    decoding, 21-22, 40, 49
    fluency, 126
    low socioeconomic children, 40
    memorization, 47, 61
    reading comprehension, 40
Word roots, 87-88
Worksheet assignments, 67-68, 75, 89
Worthy, J., 109, 140
Writing, 98-99, 129
    benchmarks, 135
    elementary grades, 112-115
    first grade, 98-99
    letters and first words, 29, 50, 91

Yopp, H. K., 33, 34, 147